A Check List of

English Plays

1641-1700

compiled by

Gertrude L. Woodward
Custodian, Rare Book Room, The Newberry Library

and

James G. McManaway
Assistant Director, The Folger Shakespeare Library

Chicago

The Newberry Library

1945

Preface

This check list began as a list of Restoration plays compiled from catalogues and bibliographies by Miss Jane D. Harding when she was a member of the Newberry Library staff. It was extended by the additions and corrections made by fifteen libraries invited to co-operate, and it was finally merged with a similar list of Civil War and Commonwealth plays undertaken at the Folger Shakespeare Library as a project of the 1942 Bibliography Committee of the seventeenth century group of the Modern Language Association of America. Its purpose is to record the plays and masques, with the variant editions and issues, printed in the English language in the British Isles or in other countries during the years 1641 to 1700, inclusive, and to give the location of copies in a number of American libraries. Though Donald G. Wing's projected "Short Title Catalogue of English Books, 1641-1700" will include these same entries, this check list may by reason of its specialized nature continue to prove useful.

Excluded from this check list are reprints of classical Greek and Latin plays in their original tongues, and political and critical dialogues which were never intended for stage presentation. Included are translations and adaptations of classical plays, a few moral and literary pieces, where there is at least a possibility that they were performed as academic or religious exercises, and royal and civic pageants, even those in which the printed text contains little more than narration or set speeches. Plays are listed alphabetically under the names of their authors, anonymous plays under their titles, with a minimum of cross references to translators and adapters. Titles and imprints, which are given in abbreviated form with the place of publication noted only if it is not London, are not repeated in the entry of latter issues and editions unless there are significant changes. References to standard bibliographies are sometimes given in parentheses. Dryden's works, it may be noted here, are more minutely described than those of even more important dramatists because of the existence of Macdonald's detailed bibliography. Individual plays in collected editions are not given separate listings, except in the case of collections of from two to five plays where each play generally has a separate title-page and independent signatures.

The symbols which designate collaborating libraries are those used in the Union Catalogue in the Library of Congress. If no copy of an item could be located in one of these libraries, either the name of at least one American or English library which possesses it is given in full or the source of the entry is indicated.

The war has affected this list in two respects. Library evacuation programs, such as the Folger's, have in some cases made it impossible to determine exactly what issues or editions of a play a library has. In such cases asterisks before the library symbol indicate a lack of specific information. And it has been thought impractical to add to the burdens of depleted library staffs by asking them to recheck this list in its completed form. Thus some omissions have doubtless occurred; these the editors regret.

One gratifying result of the compilation is the discovery that three fourths of the 1340 separate items are available to scholars in each of two libraries in America, the Folger and the Huntington, and more than half of them in each of two others, Harvard and Yale.

The compilers express deep appreciation to libraries and staffs who have cheerfully and willingly co-operated in the making of this list. Without their assistance the work would have been abandoned, for travelling difficulties made personal examination of questioned plays impossible. Gratitude for support and critical assistance is also extended to Professors R. H. Griffith of the University of Texas, Louis Bredvold of the University of Michigan, G. E. Bentley of the University of Chicago, M. A. Shaaber of the University of Pennsylvania, and R. C. Bald of Cornell University, and to Messrs. Herman R. Mead of the Henry E. Huntington Library, William A. Jackson of the Houghton Library at Harvard, William Van Lennep of the Harvard Theatre Collection, and Donald G. Wing of the Yale University Library. Likewise we thank Miss Charlotte Dobbs of the Newberry Library for helping in many ways in the preparation and editing of the manuscript.

This check list went to press several months ago. Unavoidable delays have held up publication, and in the meantime the successful prosecution of the war has permitted the return from storage of the Union Catalogue in the Library of Congress and the evacuated books of the Folger Library and of the Library of Congress. In a Supplement at the end of this book, Dr. McManaway reports a substantial number of editions and issues that had not previously been differentiated, together with the location of such copies as have been consulted in the process. We regret that it was impossible to incorporate these findings in the body of the list.

G.L.W.
J.G.M.

Co-operating Libraries

CLUC	William Andrews Clark Memorial Library, University of California at Los Angeles
CSmH	Henry E. Huntington Library, San Marino, California
CtY	Yale University Library, New Haven, Connecticut
·DFo	Folger Shakespeare Library, Washington, D. C.
DLC	Library of Congress, Washington, D. C.
ICN	Newberry Library, Chicago, Illinois
ICU	University of Chicago Library, Chicago, Illinois
IEN	Northwestern University Library, Evanston, Illinois
MH	Harvard University Library, Cambridge, Massachusetts
MWiW-C	Chapin Library, Williams College, Williamstown, Mass.
MiU	University of Michigan Library, Ann Arbor, Michigan
NIC	Cornell University Library, Ithaca, New York
NN	New York Public Library, New York City
NjP	Princeton University Library, Princeton, New Jersey
PU	University of Pennsylvania, Philadelphia, Pennsylvania
TxU	University of Texas Library, Austin, Texas

Bibliographical Citations

CBEL   Cambridge bibliography of English literature. 4 vols. 1941.

Clark   W. S. Clark, The dramatic works of Roger Boyle, Earl of Orrery. 2 vols. 1937.

DNB   Dictionary of national biography.

D and M   C. L. Day & E. B. Murrie, English songbooks, 1651-1702. A bibliography. 1940.

G   W. W. Greg, A bibliography of the English printed drama to the Restoration. Vol. I. 1939.

Greg   W. W. Greg, A list of English plays written before 1643 and printed before 1700. 1900.

Harbage   Alfred Harbage, Annals of English drama 975-1700. 1940.

Hazlitt   W. C. Hazlitt, Hand-book to the popular, poetical, and dramatic literature of Great Britain. 1867. Also Bibliographical Collections and Notes, etc.

Lowndes   W. T. Lowndes, The bibliographers manual of English literature, ed. H. G. Bohn. 6 vols. 1869.

M   Hugh Macdonald, John Dryden. A bibliography of early editions and of Drydeniana. 1939.

Nicoll   Allardyce Nicoll, A history of Restoration drama 1660-1700. 2d ed. 1928.

Osborn   James Osborn, Macdonald's Bibliography of Dryden: An annotated check list of selected American libraries, *Modern Philology* 39 (August, November, 1941), 69-98; 197-212.

P   The Carl Pforzheimer Library. English literature 1475-1700. 3 vols. 1940.

STC   A. W. Pollard and G. R. Redgrave, A short-title catalogue of books printed in England, Scotland, and Ireland and of English books printed abroad 1475-1640. 1926.

Summers   Montague Summers, A bibliography of the Restoration drama, n.d.

English Plays

1641-1700

1 A., R.
　　The valiant Welshman; or, The true chronicle history of the
　　life and valiant deeds of Caradoc the great, king of Cam-
　　bria, now called Wales. W. Gilbertson, 1663. 4°. (G327b)
　　CSmH, CtY, DFo, DLC, ICN, MH, NN.

2 ANDROMANA; or, The merchant's wife. By J. S. J. Bellin-
　　ger, 1660. 4°. CLUC, CSmH, DFo, DLC, ICN.

3 ANDRONICUS; a tragedy, Impieties long successe or heavens
　　late revenge. R. Hall, 1661. 8°. CSmH.

　ARIADNE, pseud. See *She ventures and he wins;* and *The
　　unnatural mother.*

4 ARISTOPHANES
　　Clouds, tr. T. Stanley. 1655. fol. In Stanley's *The history
　　of philosophy.* H. Moseley and T. Dring, 1655-1662. 4v. DFo.

5 - - [Anr.edn.] 1687. fol. In Stanley's *The history of philoso-
　　phy.* 1687. ICN.

　- Plutus. 1651. See Randolph, T. *Ploutophthalmia Ploutogamia.*

6 - The world's idol; or, Plutus the god of wealth. Tr. by H.H.
　　B[urnell.] W. G., sold by R. Skelton, I. Pridmore and H.
　　Marsh, 1659. 4°. CSmH, CtY, ICN, ICU, MiU.

　ARROWSMITH, JOSEPH. See *The reformation,* 1673.

　B., R. See Bernard, R.

　B.,T. See Shirley, J. *Love will finde out the way,* 1661.

　B., T. See *The rebellion of Naples,* 1649.

7 BAILEY, ABRAHAM
The spightful sister. T. Dring, the younger, 1667. 4°. CtY,
DLC, TxU.

8 - - [Anr.issue.] F. Kirkman, 1667. 4°. CSmH, DFo.

9 BANCROFT, JOHN
Henry the second, king of England; with The death of Rosa-
mond. J. Tonson, 1693. 4°. CLUC, CSmH, CtY, DFo,
DLC, ICN, ICU, MH, MiU, NIC, NjP, PU, TxU.

10 - King Edward the third, with The fall of Mortimer, Earl of
March. J. Hindmarsh, R. Bently, A. Roper, and R. Taylor,
1691. 4°. (P 39) CLUC, CSmH, CtY, DFo, DLC, ICN,
ICU, MH, MWiW-C, MiU, NjP, PU, TxU.

11 - The tragedy of Sertorius. R. Bentley and M. Magnes, 1679.
4°. (P 40) CSmH, CtY, DFo, DLC, ICN, ICU, MH,
MWiW-C, MiU, NjP, TxU.

BAND, CUFF, AND RUFF. See *A merry dialogue.*

12 THE BANISH'D DUKE; or, The tragedy of Infortunatus.
R. Baldwin, 1690. 4°. CSmH, CtY, DFo, DLC, ICN, MH,
MiU.

13 BANKS, JOHN
Cyrus the great; or, The tragedy of love. R. Bentley, 1696.
4°. CLUC, CSmH, (2 copies with variant line-endings on
p.1, lines 4-5), CtY, DFo, DLC, ICN, ICU, MH, MiU, NIC,
NjP, TxU.

14 - The destruction of Troy. A. G. and J. P., sold by C. Blount,
1679. 4°. CSmH, CtY, DFo, DLC, ICN, ICU, MH,
MWiW-C, MiU, NjP, TxU.

15 - The innocent usurper; or, The death of the Lady Jane Gray.
R. Bentley, 1694. 4°. CSmH, CtY, DFo, DLC, ICN, ICU,
MH, MiU, NIC, NjP.

2

BANKS, JOHN (continued)

16   The island queens; or, The death of Mary Queen of Scotland.
R. Bentley, 1684. 4°. CSmH, CtY, DLC, ICN, ICU, MH,
MiU, NjP, TxU.

17   - The rival kings; or, The loves of Oroondates and Statira. L.
Curtis, 1677. 4° CLUC, CSmH, CtY, DLC, ICN, ICU,
MH, MiU, TxU.

18   - - [Anr.issue.]L. C., 1677. 4°. DFo, DLC, ICN.

19   - The unhappy favourite; or, The earl of Essex. R. Bentley
and M. Magnes, 1682. 4°. CLUC, CSmH, CtY, DFo,
DLC, ICN, ICU, MH, MWiW-C, NjP.

20   - - [Anr.edn.] 1685. 4°. CLUC, CSmH, CtY, DFo, MiU,
TxU.

21   - - [Anr.edn.] R. Bentley, 1693. 4°. CtY, DFo, MH, MiU.

22   - - [Anr.edn.] R. Wellington, [1699.] 4°. ICU, MiU.

23   - Vertue betray'd; or, Anna Bullen. R. Bentley and M. Magnes,
1682. 4°. CLUC, CSmH, CtY, DFo, DLC, ICN, ICU,
MH, MWiW-C, MiU, NIC, NjP, TxU.

24   - - [Anr.edn.] R. Bentley, 1692. 4°. DFo, ICN, MH.

25   BARON, ROBERT
An apologie for Paris. T. Dring, 1649. 8°. DFo, ICN.

26   – Deorum dona. I :H. T :H. T :I.,1647. 8°. Interpolated masque in his *Erotopaignion; or, The Cyprian academy,* 1647.
CSmH, DFo.

27   - - [Anr.issue.] 1647. 8°. In his *Erotopaignion; or, The Cyprian academy,* 1648. CLUC, CSmH, CtY, DFo, DLC, ICN,
MH, MWiW-C.

BARON, ROBERT (continued)

28   Gripus and Hegio; or, The passionate lovers. 8°. Interpolated masque in his *Erotopaignion; or, The Cyprian academy,* 1647. CSmH.

29   - - [Anr.issue.]   In his *Erotopaignion; or, The Cyprian academy,* 1648.   CLUC, CSmH, CtY, DFo, DLC, ICN, MH, MWiW-C.

30   - Mirza.   A tragedie, really acted in Persia, in the last age. H. Moseley and T. Dring, [1655?]   8°.   (P 43)   CLUC, CSmH, CtY, DFo, DLC, ICN, MH, MWiW-C, NIC, PU.

31   BEAUMONT, FRANCIS.   See also Beaumont, Francis and John Fletcher.
A maske of the gentlemen of Graies Inne, and the Inner Temple. 1653. 8°. (G 309c)   In his *Poems,* W. Hope, 1653. CLUC, DFo.

32   - - [Anr.issue.]   (G 309c)   In his *Poems,* L. Blaiklock, 1653. CSmH, CtY, ICN, ICU, MH.

33   - - [Anr.issue.] In his *Poems. The golden remains,* 1660. CtY, DFo, ICN, NN.

34   BEAUMONT, FRANCIS and JOHN FLETCHER
Comedies and tragedies.   H. Robinson and H. Moseley, 1647. fol. (P 53)   CLUC, CSmH, CtY, DFo, DLC, ICN, ICU, MH, MWiW-C, MiU, NIC, NN, NjP, PU, TxU.

35   - Fifty comedies and tragedies.   J. Macock for J. Martyn, H. Herringman, R. Marriot, 1679. fol. (P 54)   CLUC, CSmH, CtY, DFo, DLC, ICN, ICU, IEN, MH, MWiW-C, MiU, NIC, NjP, PU, TxU.

36   - The beggars bush.   H. Robinson, and A. Mosely, 1661.   4°. MH.

37   - - [Anr.issue.]   CSmH, DFo, MH.
With warning against Kirkman on title.

BEAUMONT, FRANCIS and JOHN FLETCHER (cont.)
Bonduca; or, The British heroine. 1696. See Powell, G.

- The chances. 1682. See Villiers, G .

38 - The elder brother. H. Moseley, 1650. 4°. CtY,

39 - - [Anr.issue.] H. Moseley, 1651. 4°. CSmH, CtY, DFo,
DLC, ICN, MH, TxU.
"The second edition, corrected and amended."

40 - - [Anr.edn.] Printed in the year, 1661. 4°. CSmH, CtY.
DFo, DLC, ICU, MH, TxU.

41 - - [Anr.edn.] T.N. for D.N. and T.C. and sold by G. Marriott,
1678. 4°. CSmH, DFo, MH.

42 - The faithfull shepherdesse. G. Bedell and T. Collins, 1656. 4°.
(G 287d) CSmH, DFo, DLC, MH.

43 - - [Anr.edn.] G. Bedell and T. Collins, 1665. 4°. (G 287e)
CLUC, CSmH, DFo, MH.

44 - - [Anr.edn., tr. into Latin by Richard Fanshawe] Fida pastora. Typis R. Danielis, impensis G. Bedell & T. Collins, 1658.
8°. CSmH, ICU, MH.

45 - Fathers own son. R.Crofts, [c.1661.] 4°. CSmH.
Re-issue of *Monsieur Thomas*, 1639, with cancel title.

46 - The humorous lieutenant; or, Generous enemies. H.N. and
sold by W. Chandler and R. Smith, 1697. 4°. DFo, ICU, MH.
Anonymous adaptation.

47 - The island princess; or, The generous Portugal. H.R. and
A.M. and sold by W. Cademan and R. Pask, 1669. 4°. CLUC,
CtY, DFo, DLC, ICN, MH, MiU.
Anonymous adaptation.

- - [Anr.edn.]   1687.   See Tate, N.

- - [Anr.edn.]   1699.   See Motteux, P.A.

48 - A king and no king.   W. Leak, 1655.   4°.   CLUC, CSmH,
DFo, DLC, TxU.

49 - - [Anr.edn.]   Printed in the year 1661.   4°.   CSmH, CtY,
DFo, MH.

50 - - [Anr.edn.]   A. Clark for W. and J. Leake, 1676.   4°.   CtY,
DFo, ICU, MH, NN, NjP, TxU.

51 - - [Anr.edn.]   R. Bentley, 1693.   4°.   CSmH, CtY, DFo, MH,
TxU.

52 - The knight of the burning pestle.   N.O. for I.S.,1635.   4°.
(STC 1675a; P 49)   CSmH, DFo, MH.
    A falsely dated edition, with the spelling Beamount (or
    Beaumount) on the title-page.   Probably printed between
    1650 and 1661.

53 - The loyal subject; or, The faithful general.   H.N. to be sold by
W.Keble, [1700?]   4°.   DFo, MH.

54 - The maids tragedie.   E.P. for W.Leake,1641.   4°.   CSmH,
DFo, MH.

55 - - [Anr.edn.]   W. Leake, 1650.   4°.   CSmH, DFo, DLC, MH.

56 - - [Anr.edn.]   Printed in the year 1661.   4°.   DFo, DLC, MH.

57 - - [Anr.edn.]   R. Bentley and S. Magnes, 1686.   4°.   DFo,
ICN, ICU, MH.

- - [Anr.edn.]   1690.   See Waller, E.   *The maid's tragedy
altered.*

- Monsieur Thomas.   See Beaumont, F. and J.Fletcher. *Fathers
own son.*

58 The night-walker; or, The little thief. A. Crook, 1661. 4°.
CSmH, DFo, DLC, ICU, MH, NjP.

59 - Philaster; or, Love lies a bleeding. W. Leake, 1652. 4°. CtY,
DFo, MH.
A double row of fleurs-de-lys on the title-page.

60 - - [Anr.edn.] W.Leake,1652. 4°. CSmH, DFo.
A list of books on verso of title-page.

61 - - [Anr.edn.] W. Leake, [1661?] 4°. CSmH, DFo, DLC,
ICU, MH.

62 - - [Anr.edn.] R. Bentley and S. Magnes, 1687. 4°. CtY, DFo,
ICU, MH.

- - [Anr.edn.] 1695. See Settle, E.

- The pilgrim. 1700. See Vanbrugh, J.

- The prophetess; or, The history of Dioclesian. 1690. See
Betterton, T.

63 - Rollo, Duke of Normandy; or, The bloody brother. R.Holt for
D.Newman,1686. 4°. DFo, ICU, MH, NIC.

64 - Rule a wife, and have a wife. S.Briscoe and sold by R.Wel-
lington, 1697. 4°. CSmH, DFo.

65 The scornefull lady. H. Moseley, 1651. 4°. (G 334f) CSmH,
DFo, MH.
"The sixt Edition, Corrected and amended."

66 - - [Anr.edn.] H. Moseley, 1651. 4°. (G 334g) DFo.
"The sixt Edition, Corrected and Amended." Greg conjectures that this may have been published "some years
after the date on the title."

BEAUMONT, FRANCIS and JOHN FLETCHER (cont.)

67 - - [Anr.edn.]   H. Moseley, 1651. 4°. (G 334h) CSmH, CtY, DFo, MH.
 "The sixt Edition, Corrected and amended." Greg conjectures that this edition is later than 334g.

68 - - [Anr.edn.]   A. Maxwell and R. Roberts, for D. N. and T. C., and sold by L. Curtis, 1677. 4°. (G 334iI) DFo, MH.

69 - - [Anr.issue with cancel title.]   A. Maxwell and R. Roberts for D. N. and T. C., and sold by S. Neale, 1677. 4°. (G 334iII) DFo, MH.

70 - - [Anr.edn.]   D. Newman, 1691. 4°. (G 334k) DFo, MH.

71 - - [Anr.edn.]   J. T. and sold by G. Harris and J. Graves, J. Barnes, D. Newman, J. Harding, W. Lewis and T. Archer, B. Lintot and E. Sanger, J. Knapton, R. Smith and G. Strahan, [1695?] 4°. (G 334 1) CSmH, DFo, ICU.

72 - The tragedy of Thierry King of France, and his brother Theodoret. H. Mosely, 1648. 4°. CSmH, DFo, MH.

73 - - [Anr.issue.]   H. Moseley, 1649.   4°.   CSmH, CtY, DFo, ICN, ICU, MH, TxU.

74 Entry cancelled.

 - Valentinian.   1685.   See Wilmot, J.

75 - The wild-goose chase.   H. Moseley, 1652. fol. (P 52) CLUC, CSmH, CtY, DFo, DLC, ICU, MH, MWiW-C, MiU, TxU.

76 - Wit without money.   A. Crooke, 1661.   4°.   CSmH, CtY, DFo, MH.

77 The woman hater.   H. Moseley, 1648. 4°. (G 245bI) CSmH, CtY, DFo, DLC, ICU, MH.

8

BEAUMONT, FRANCIS and JOHN FLETCHER (continued)
78 - - [Anr.issue, with cancel title.] H. Moseley, 1649. 4°.
    (G 245bII) CLUC, CSmH, DFo, DLC, ICU, MH, NjP,
    TxU.

79 BEHN, APHRA
    Abdelazer; or, The Moor's revenge. J. Magnes and R. Bent-
    ley, 1677. 4°. CLUC, CSmH, CtY, DFo, DLC, ICN, ICU,
    MH, NN, NjP.

80 - - [Anr.edn.] T. Chapman, 1693. 4°. CtY, DFo, MH, MiU,
    TxU.

81 - The amorous prince; or, The curious husband. J. M. for T.
    Dring, 1671. 4°. CLUC, CSmH, CtY, DFo, DLC, ICN,
    MH, NjP, TxU.

82 - The city-heiress; or, Sir Timothy Treat-all. D.Brown, T.Ben-
    skin and H. Rhodes, 1682. 4°. CLUC, CSmH, CtY, DFo,
    DLC, ICN, ICU, MH, MWiW-C, NN, NjP, TxU.

83 - - [Anr.edn.] R.Wellington,1698. 4°. MH.

84 - - [Anr.issue] R. Wellington and sold by P. Gilborne and
    B.Lintott,1698. 4°. DFo.

85 - The counterfeit bridegroom ; or, The defeated widow. L.Curtiss,
    1677. 4°. (P 701) CSmH, CtY, DFo, DLC, ICN, ICU,
    MH, NN, NjP.

86 - The debauchee; or, The credulous cuckold. J. Amery, 1677.
    4°. CLUC, CSmH, CtY, DFo, DLC, ICN, ICU, MH,
    MWiW-C.

87 - The Dutch lover. T. Dring, 1673. 4°. CLUC, CSmH, CtY,
    DFo, DLC, ICN, ICU, MH, MWiW-C, NjP, TxU.

88 - The emperor of the moon. R. Holt for J. Knight and F. Saun-
    ders, 1687. 4°. CSmH, CtY, DFo, ICU, MII, NN.

89 - - [Anr.edn.]   1688. 4°. CLUC, CSmH, CtY, DFo, DLC, MH.

90 - The false count; or,A new way to play an old game. M.Flesher for J. Tonson, 1682. 4°. CLUC, CSmH, CtY, DFo, DLC, ICN, MH, MWiW-C, NN, NjP.

91 - -[Anr.issue.]   J. Tonson, 1697. 4°. DFo, MH.

92 - The feign'd curtizans; or, A nights intrigue. J.Tonson,1679. 4°. CLUC, CSmH, CtY, DFo, DLC, ICN, ICU, MH, MWiW-C, NN, NjP, TxU.

93 - The forc'd marriage; or, The jealous bridegroom. H. L. and R. B. for J. Magnes, 1671. 4°. CLUC, CSmH, CtY, DFo, **MH.**

94 - - [Anr.edn.] J. Knapton, 1688. 4°. CSmH, CtY, DFo, DLC, ICN, MH, TxU.

95 - - [Anr.edn.] 1690. 4°. British Museum.

96 - The luckey chance; or, An alderman's bargain. R. H. for W. Canning, 1687. 4°. CLUC, CSmH, CtY, DFo, DLC, ICN, ICU, MH, MWiW-C, NjP.

- The revenge. 1677. See Betterton, T.

97 - The roundheads; or, The good old cause. D. Brown, T. Benskin and H. Rhodes, 1682. 4°. CSmH, CtY, DLC, ICN, MH. Dedication: To the Right noble Henry Fitz-Roy.

98 - - [Anr.issue.] CLUC, CSmH, DFo, MWiW-C, MiU. Dedication: To the most illustrious Prince Henry Fitz-Roy.

99 - - [Anr.edn.] R. Wellington, sold by P. Gilborne and B. Lintott, 1698. 4°. DFo, ICN, MH, NIC.

BEHN, APHRA (continued)
100 - The rover; or, The banish't cavaliers. J. Amery, 1677. 4°.
   CSmH, DFo, ICU, TxU.
      Title conjugate with [A4].

101 - - [Anr.issue.] (P 56) CLUC, *CtY, DFo, *DLC, ICN, MH,
   MWiW-C, NjP, TxU.
      Title, a cancel, adds the words, "A Comedy." Post-script
      has 19 lines.

102 - - [Anr.issue.] CSmH.
      With author's name on title-page. Post-script has 20 lines.

103 - - [Anr.edn.] J. Orme for R. Wellington, 1697. 4°. CtY,
   DFo, MH.

104 - The second part of the rover. J.Tonson,1681. 4°. CLUC,
   CSmH, CtY, DFo, DLC, ICN, ICU, MH, NN, NjP, TxU.

105 - Sir Patient Fancy. E. Flesher for R. Tonson and J. Tonson,
   1678. 4°. CLUC, CSmH, CtY, DFo, DLC, ICN, ICU, MH,
   MWiW-C, NjP, TxU.

106 - - [Anr.edn.] [1681?] CBEL II, 417.

107 - The town-fopp; or, Sir Timothy Tawdrey. T. N. for J. Magnes and R. Bentley, 1677. 4°. CLUC, CSmH, CtY, DFo,
   DLC, ICN, ICU, IEN, MH, MWiW-C, NN, NjP, TxU.

108 - - [Anr.edn.] R. Wellington, B. Lintott and E. Rumbold, 1699.
   4°. DFo.

109 - The widdow ranter; or, The history of Bacon in Virginia. J.
   Knapton, 1690. 4°. CLUC, CSmH, CtY, DFo, DLC, ICN,
   MH, MWiW-C, NN, NjP, TxU.

110 - The young king; or, The mistake. D. Brown, T. Benskin and
   H. Rhodes, 1683. 4°. CLUC, CSmH, CtY, DFo, DLC, ICN,
   ICU, MH, MWiW-C, NN.

BEHN, APHRA (continued)

111 - - [Anr.edn.] R. Wellington, sold by P. Gilborne and B. Lintott, 1698. 4°. DFo.

112 The younger brother; or, The amorous jilt. J. Harris, sold by R. Baldwin, 1696. 4°. CLUC, CSmH, CtY, DFo, DLC, ICN, ICU, MH, MWiW-C, NIC, NjP.

113 BELLON, PETER
The mock-duellist; or, The French vallet. J. C. for W. Crooke, 1675. 4°. CSmH, CtY, DFo, DLC, ICN, ICU, MH, MiU.

BERNARD, RICHARD. See Terentius Afer, P.

BETTERTON, THOMAS.
Appius and Virginia. See Webster, J.

- The counterfeit bridegroom. See Behn, Aphra.

- King Henry IV. See Shakespeare, W.

114 The prophetess; or, The history of Dioclesian. J. Tonson, 1690. 4°. (M 123) DFo.
"FINIS" on p. 74. Prologue by Dryden.

115 - - [Anr.issue, omitting prologue] (M 123) CLUC, CSmH, DFo.

116 - - [Anr.issue.] CLUC, CSmH, CtY, DFo, DLC, ICN, MH, MiU, NjP, TxU.
"FINIS" on p. [76]; "EPILOGUE" on last leaf.

117 - The revenge; or, A match in Newgate. W. Cademan, 1680. 4°. CLUC, CSmH, CtY, DFo, ICN, ICU, MH, TxU.

118 BONARELLI DELLA ROVERE, GUIDO UBALDO
Filli di Sciro; or, Phillis of Scyros. Translated by J[onathan] S[idnam.] J. M. for A. Crook, 1655. 4°. CSmH, ICU, MH.

BONDUCA. See Powell, G.

119 BOOTHBY, FRANCES
Marcelia; or, The treacherous friend. W. Cademan and G.
Widdowes, 1670. 4°. CLUC, CSmH, CtY, DFo, DLC, ICN,
ICU, MH, MWiW-C, MiU, NjP, PU, TxU.

BOTTOM THE WEAVER. See *The merry conceited humors
of Bottom the weaver*.

120 BOURNE, REUBEN
The contented cuckold; or, The womans advocate. R.Taylor,
1692. 4°. CSmH, DFo, DLC, ICN, MH, MiU.

121 BOYER, ABEL
Achilles; or, Iphigenia in Aulis. T. Bennet, 1700. 4°. CSmH,
DFo, DLC, ICU, MH, MiU.

122 BOYLE, ROGER, Earl of Orrery
Two new tragedies; The black prince and Tryphon. T. N. for
H. Herringman, 1669. fol. (Clark I, 1669, folio F1) CLUC,
CSmH, CtY, DFo, ICU, MH, NN, TxU.
Signed A-P², [Q¹], R², A-Q²; *Tryphon* has separate title-
page with same imprint. Also issued as part of *Four new
plays*, 1670.

123 - - [Anr.edn.] H. Herringman, 1672. fol. (Clark 2, 1672, folio
F2) CSmH, CtY, DFo, DLC, ICN, ICU, MH, MiU, NjP,
TxU.

124 - Four new plays; viz. The history of Henry the fifth, Mustapha,
The black prince, and Tryphon. H. Herringman, 1670. fol.
(Clark I, 1670, folio) DFo, ICN, ICU, MH, NIC, TxU.
A general title-page prefixed to a nonce collection of plays:
(1) *The history of Henry the fifth, and The tragedy of
Mustapha*, 1669; and (2) *Two new tragedies*, 1669.

125 - Six plays; viz. The history of Henry V and The tragedy of
Mustapha. The black prince and Tryphon, Herod the great,
and Guzman. H. H. and sold by F. Saunders, 1694. fol.
(Clark 2, 1694, folio) CLUC.

A general title-page prefixed to a nonce collection consisting frequently of (1) *The history of Henry V and The tragedy of Mustapha,* 1690; (2) *The black prince and Tryphon,* 1672; (3) *Herod the great* (one of the issues of 1694); and (4) *Guzman,* 1693.

\- The black prince. See his *Two new tragedies,* 1669; *Four new plays,* 1670; and *Six plays,* 1694.

126 - Guzman. F. Saunders, 1693. fol. (Clark I, 1693, folio) CtY, DFo, DLC, ICN, ICU, MH, NjP.
See also his *Six plays,* 1694.

127 - Herod the great. T. Warren for F. Saunders and T. Bennet, 1694. fol. (Clark IA, 1694, folio) DLC, MH.
See also his *Six plays,* 1694.

128 - - [Anr.issue.] T. Warren for F. Saunders, T. Bennet, and J. Knapton, 1694. fol. (Clark IB, 1694, folio) DFo, ICN.
See also his *Six plays,* 1694.

129 - The history of Henry the fifth, and The tragedy of Mustapha, son of Solyman the magnificent. H. Herringman, 1668. fol. (Clark I, 1668, folio F1) *CSmH, *CtY (Henry the fifth only), DFo, MiU (Henry the fifth only), TxU.
Signed Aa-Oo²; A-T².

130 - - [Anr.edn.] 1668. fol. (Clark 2, 1668, folio F2) DFo, ICN.
Signed A-Z², Aa-Ii².

131 - - [Anr.edn.] T. N. for H. Herringman, 1669. fol. (Clark 3, 1669, folio F3) CSmH, CtY, DFo, ICU, NN, TxU.
Issued also as part of *Four new plays.* 1670.

132 - - [Anr.edn.] J. M. for H. Herringman, 1672. fol. (Clark 4, 1672, folio F4) ICU, MH.

133 - - [Anr.edn.] T. N. for H. Herringman, 1677. fol. (Clark 5, 1677, folio F5) CSmH, CtY, DFo, DLC.

14

BOYLE, ROGER, Earl of Orrery (continued)
134 - - [Anr.edn.]   H. Herringman, and sold by J. Knight, 1690.
fol. (Clark 6, 1690, folio F6) CSmH, CtY, DFo, DLC, MH,
MiU (Mustapha only).

135 - Mr. Anthony. J. Knapton, 1690. 4°. (Clark IA, 1690, quarto)
*CSmH, *CtY, MH.
   Date reads "MDCXC."

136 - - [Anr.issue.] 1690. 4°. (Clark IB, 1690, quarto) DFo,
DLC, TxU.

- Mustapha. See his *The history of Henry the fifth, and The
tragedy of Mustapha.*

- The tragedy of Mustapha. See his *The history of Henry the
fifth, and The tragedy of Mustapha.*

- Tryphon. See his *Two new tragedies,* 1669; *Four new plays,*
1670; *Six plays,* 1694.

137 BRADY, NICHOLAS
   The rape; or, The innocent impostors. R.Bentley,1692. 4°.
   CSmH, DFo, DLC, ICN, ICU, MiU.

138 - - [Anr.issue.]   S. Crouch, 1692. 4°. DFo.

139 - - [Anr.issue.]   F. Bennet, 1692. 4°. DFo, NjP.

140 - - [Anr.issue.]   F. Saunders, 1692. 4°. CSmH, DFo.

141 THE BRAGADOCIO; or, The bawd turn'd puritan. R. Baldwin, 1691. 4°. CSmH, DFo, DLC, ICN, MH, MiU, TxU.

142 BRATHWAIT, RICHARD
   Mercurius Britannicus. Judicialis censura; vel, curialis cura.
   Febris judicialis. Sententia navilis. Tragi-comoedia Lutetiae.
   n.p.,n.d., [1641?] 4°. CtY, DFo.
      Signed A-D⁴.

BRATHWAIT, RICHARD (continued)
143 - - [Anr.edn.] [1641?] 4°. DFo, ICN, PU.
    Signed A1-2, *², A3-4, B-D⁴. "Editio secunda."

144 - - [Anr.edn. with changed title.] Mercurius Britanicus, or The
    English intelligencer. Printed in the yeare, 1641. 4°. CLUC,
    CSmH, CtY, DFo, ICU, MH.
    Signed A-D⁴, E².

145 - - [Anr.edn.] Printed in the yeare, 1641. 4°. DLC (imper-
    fect).
    Signed A-D⁴.

146 - - [Anr.edn.] Printed in the yeare, 1641. 4°. CSmH, ICN,
    TxU.
    Signed A-C⁴, D².

147 - - [Anr.edn.] 1641. 4°. (P 80, note)
    Signed A⁴, a², B-C⁴, D².

148 BREWER, ANTHONY
    The countrie girle. A. R., 1647. 4°. CLUC, CSmH, CtY,
    DFo, DLC, ICN, ICU, MH.

149 - The love-sick king, an English tragical history; with the life
    and death of Cartesmunda, the fair nun of Winchester. R.
    Pollard and J. Sweeting, 1655. 4°. CLUC, CSmH, CtY,
    DFo, DLC, ICN, ICU, MiU, PU.

150 - - [Anr.edn. with changed title.] The perjured nun. 1680. 4°.
    (CBEL I, 641).

151 BREWER, THOMAS
    A knot of fooles. F. Grove, 1658. 4°. CSmH, DFo.

152 BROME, ALEXANDER
    The cunning lovers. W. Sheares, 1654. 4°. CLUC, CSmH,
    CtY, DFo, DLC, ICN, ICU, MH, MiU.

153 BROME, RICHARD

Five new playes; viz. The madd couple well matcht. The novella. The court begger. The city witt. The damoiselle. H. Moseley, R. Marriot, and T. Dring, 1653. 8°. (P 107) CLUC, CSmH, DFo, DLC, ICN, ICU, NjP, NN, TxU.

Novella and *Court begger* have separate title-pages with imprint: R. Marriot and T. Dring, 1653. *City wit* and *Damoiselle* have separate title-pages with imprint: T. R. for R. Mariot and T. Dring, 1653.

154 Entry cancelled.

155 - - [Anr.issue.] J. F. and sold by J. Sweeting, 1654. 8°. CtY.

156 - Five new playes, viz. The English moor, or, The mock-marriage. The love-sick court; or, The ambitious politique. Covent Garden weeded. The new academy; or, The new exchange. The queen and concubine. A. Crook and H. Brome, 1659. 8°. CSmH, CtY, DFo, DLC, ICU.

The first two plays have continuous signatures and pagination; the third and fourth plays have continuous signatures but independent pagination; the fifth play has independent signatures and pagination.

157 - - [Anr.issue.] CLUC, CSmH, CtY, ICN, *MH, MWiW-C, NIC, *NN.

In this issue a cancel title-page for *English moor* with imprint, "Printed in the year, 1659," replaces the original, with imprint, "J. T. for A. C. and H. Broom, 1658;" and *New academy* and *Covent Garden* have new imprints, "A. Crook and H. Brome, 1658," instead of "A. Crook, 1658."

- The city witt. See his *Five new playes*, 1653.

- The court begger. See his *Five new playes*, 1653.

- Covent Garden weeded. See his *Five new playes*, 1659.

- The damoiselle. See his *Five new playes*, 1653.

BROME, RICHARD (continued)
The English moor. See his *Five new playes,* 1659.

158 - A joviall crew; or, The merry beggars. J.Y. for E.D. and
N.E., 1652. 4°. CLUC, CSmH, CtY, DFo, DLC, ICU,
MH, MWiW-C, TxU.

159 - - [Anr.edn.] H. Brome, 1661. 4°. DFo, ICN, MH.

160 - - [Anr.edn.] J. Hindmarsh, 1684. 4°. CSmH, CtY, DFo,
ICN, MH.

- The love-sick court. See his *Five new playes,* 1659.

- The madd couple well matcht. See his *Five new playes,* 1653.

- The new academy. See his *Five new playes,* 1659.

161 - The northern lasse. A. Moseley, 1663. 4°. CSmH.

162 - - [Anr.edn.] D. Newman, 1684. 4°. CSmH, CtY, DFo, DLC,
MH, PU, TxU.

163 - - [Anr.edn.] [W. Kehle, 1700] 4°. British Museum (lacks
title).

- The novella. See his *Five new playes,* 1653.

- The queen and concubine. See his *Five new playes,* 1659.

164 - The queenes exchange. H. Brome, 1657. 4°. (P 108) CSmH,
DFo, DLC, ICN, MH, NjP, TxU.

165 - - [Anr.issue with cancel title.] The royall exchange. H. Brome,
1661. 4°. CSmH, CtY.

- The weeding of Covent-Garden. See *Covent Garden weeded*
in his *Five new playes,* 1659.

166 BROWN, THOMAS
   Physick lies a bleeding; or, The apothecary turned doctor.
   E. Whitlock, 1697. 4°. CSmH, CtY, DLC, ICU, MiU, TxU

167 BUCHANAN, GEORGE
   Tyrannicall-government anatomized; or, A discourse concern-
   ing evil-councellors. J.Field,1642. 4°. CLUC, CSmH, CtY,
   DFo, ICN, MH.
      Translation by J. Milton (?) of *Baptistes sive calumnia*.

168 BULTEEL, JOHN
   Amorous Orontus; or, The love in fashion. G. M. for J. Playfere, 1665. 4°. CSmH, NIC.
      Translated from T. Corneille.

169 - - [Anr.edn. with changed title.] The amorous gallant; or, Love
   in fashion. J. C. for W. Crook, 1675. 4°. CSmH, CtY,
   DFo, DLC, ICN, ICU, MH, MiU, NjP.

170 - Londons triumph; or, The solemn and magnificent reception of
   Robert Tichburn, lord major, October 29, 1656. N. Brook,
   1656. 4°. CSmH.

171 BURKHEAD, HENRY
   The tragedy of Cola's fury; or, Lirenda's misery. Kilkenny,
   T. Bourke, 1645. To be sould 1646. 4°. British Museum.

172 BURNABY, WILLIAM
   The reform'd wife. T. Bennet, 1700. 4°. CLUC, CSmH,
   CtY, DFo (2 variants), DLC, ICN, ICU, MH, MWiW-C,
   NIC, NjP, TxU.

173 - - [Anr.issue, with cancel title-page.] CtY, DFo, DLC (imperfect), ICN, ICU, MiU.
      "The second edition."

174 BURNELL, HENRY
   Landgartha; or, The Amazon queen of Denmark. Printed at
   Dublin, 1641. 4°. CSmH, MH.

   - The world's idol. See Aristophanes.

C., J. See *A pleasant comedy called The two merry milkmaids.*

175 CANCER. Typis R. C. sumptibus A. Crooks, 1648. 12°. In
Hackett, J., *Loiola,* 1648. CtY, DFo, ICN, MH.

176 CAREW, THOMAS
Coelum Brittanicum. T. Walkley, 1642. 8°. (P 128) In his
Poems, I. D. for T. Walkley, 1642. CLUC, CSmH, CtY,
DFo, ICN, ICU, MH, MWiW-C.

177 - - [Anr.edn.] H. M., 1651. 8°. In his *Poems, with a maske,*
1651. See P 129, note.

178 - - [Anr.issue] H. Moseley, 1651. 8°. In his *Poems, with a*
maske. H. M. and sold by J. Martin, 1651. (P 129) CLUC,
CSmH, CtY, DFo, ICN, MH.

179 - - [Anr.edn.] In the Savoy for H. Herringman, 1670. 8°. In
his *Poems, songs and sonnets, together with a masque,* 1670.
CLUC, CSmH, DFo, ICN, MH, NjP.
See P 130.

180 - - [Anr.issue.] In his *Poems, songs and sonnets, together with*
a masque. H. Herringman, and sold by H. Kemp, 1671.
(P 130) CSmH, DFo, MH.

181 - - [Anr.edn.] In Davenant, W. *Works.* T. N. for H. Herringman, 1673. fol. CLUC, CSmH, CtY, DFo, DLC, ICN, ICU,
MH, NIC, TxU.

182 CARLELL, LODOWICK
Two new playes. Viz. 1. The fool would be a favourit; or,
The discreet lover. 2. Osmond, the great Turk; or, The noble
servant. H. Moseley, 1657. 8°. CLUC, CSmH, CtY, DFo,
DLC, ICN, ICU, MH, PU (Fool would be a favourit only),
TxU.

183 - The deserving favorite. H. Moseley, 1659. 8°. CSmH, CtY,
DFo, DLC, ICN, MH, NjP, PU.

- The fool would be a favourit. See his *Two new playes.* 1657.
20

CARLELL, LODOWICK (continued)

184 - Heraclius, emperour of the East. J. Starkey, 1664. 4°. CSmH,
CtY, DFo, DLC, ICN, MH, NIC, NN, PU, TxU.
Translated from P. Corneille.

- Osmond, the great Turk. See his *Two new playes,* 1657.

185 - The passionate lovers. H. Moseley, 1655. 4°. CLUC, CSmH,
ICU, MH, MiU, NjP, PU, TxU.

186 - - [Anr.edn.] H. Moseley, 1655. 8°. CSmH, CtY, DFo, DLC,
ICN, NIC.

187 CARLISLE, JAMES
The fortune-hunters; or, Two fools well met. J. Knapton,
1689. 4°. CLUC, CSmH, CtY, DFo, ICN, ICU, MH,
MWiW-C, MiU, NjP, TxU.

188 CARPENTER, RICHARD
A new play call'd the pragmatical Jesuit new-leven'd. N. R.
[1661 or 1665.] 4°. (P 132) CSmH, CtY, DFo, DLC,
ICN, ICU, MH, MWiW-C, MiU, PU.

CARROLL, SUSANNA. See Centlivre, Susanna.

189 CARTWRIGHT, GEORGE
The heroick-lover. P. W. for J. Symmes, 1661. 8°. CLUC,
CtY, DLC, MH.

190 CARTWRIGHT, WILLIAM
Comedies, tragi-comedies, with other poems. H. Moseley, 1651.
8°. CLUC, CSmH, CtY, DFo, DLC, ICN, ICU, IEN, MH,
MWiW-C, MiU, NN, PU, TxU.
See *The Library* 4 ser. XXIII, 12-22; *The Library Quart-
erly* XII, 438-56.

- The lady errant. See his *Comedies, tragi-comedies, with other
poems,* 1651.

CARTWRIGHT, WILLIAM (continued)
The ordinary. See his *Comedies, tragi-comedies, with other poems,* 1651.

- The royall slave. T. R. and H. Moseley, 1651 See his *Comedies, tragi-comedies, with other poems,* 1651.

- The siedge; or, Love's convert. See his *Comedies, tragi-comedies, with other poems,* 1651.

191 CARY, HENRY, Viscount Falkland
The mariage night. W. G. for R. Crofts, 1664. 4°. (P 134)
CSmH, DFo, DLC, ICN, ICU, MH, MiU.

192 CARYLL, JOHN
The English princess; or, The death of Richard the III. T. Dring, 1667. 4°. (P 135) *CLUC, *CSmH, *CTY, DFo, ICN, ICU, *MH, *MWiW-C, *MiU, TxU.
"St. Dunstans-Church" in imprint.

193 - - [Anr.issue] DFo, DLC, TxU.
"Cliffords-Inn" in imprint.

194 - - [Anr.edn.] R. B. for T. Basset, 1673. 4°. CLUC, PU.

195 - - [Anr.edn.] R. B. for T. Basset, sold by W. Cademan, 1674. 4°. CtY, DFo, ICU, NjP, TxU.

196 - Sir Salomon; or, The cautious coxcomb. H. Herringman, 1671. 4°. (P 136) CLUC, CSmH, CtY, DFo, DLC, ICN, ICU, MH, MWiW-C, MiU, NN, NjP, TxU.

197 - - [Anr.edn.] H. Herringman, 1691. 4°. CtY, NjP.

198 - - [Anr.issue.] H. Herringman, sold by J. Tonson, 1691. 4°. DFo, DLC, MH, NN.

199 CAVENDISH, MARGARET, Duchess of Newcastle
Playes. A. Warren for J. Martyn, J. Allestry and T. Dicas, 1662. fol. (P 138) CLUC, CSmH, CtY, DFo, ICN, ICU, MH, MWiW-C, MiU, NjP.

200 - Plays, never before printed. A. Maxwell, 1668. fol.. (P 139) CLUC, CSmH, CtY, DFo, ICN, ICU, MH, MiU.

201 CAVENDISH, WILLIAM, Duke of Newcastle
The country captaine, and The varietie, two comedies. H. Robinson and H. Moseley, 1649. 12°. CSmH, DFo, DLC, ICN, MH, PU, TxU.

-The country captaine. In's Grave van Haghe. S. Broun, 1649. See his *The country captaine, and The varietie, two comedies,* 1649.

202 - The humorous lovers. J. M. for H. Herringman, 1677. 4°. CSmH, CtY, DFo, DLC, ICN, ICU, MH, MWiW-C, MiU, NjP, TxU.

- Sir Martin Mar-all. See Dryden, J.

203 - The triumphant widow; or, The medley of humours. J. M. for H. Herringman, 1677. 4°. CSmH, CtY, DFo, DLC, ICN, ICU, MH, MWiW-C, MiU, TxU.

- The varietie. H. Moseley, 1649. See his *The country captaine, and The varietie, two comedies,* 1649.

204 CENTLIVRE, SUSANNA
The perjur'd husband; or, The adventures of Venice. B. Banbury, 1700. 4°. CLUC, CSmH, CtY, DFo, DLC, ICN, ICU, MH, MWiW-C, MiU, NjP, TxU.

205 CHAMBERLAINE, WILLIAM
Love's victory. E. Cotes and sold by R. Clavell, 1658. 4°. CSmH, DFo, DLC, ICN, ICU, MWiW-C, PU, TxU.

- Wits led by the nose. See under title.

206 CHAPMAN, GEORGE

    Comedies, tragi-comedies; & tragedies. Printed Ann: Dom: 1652. 4°. CSmH.

    Title-page of a nonce collection, now broken up, of six pre-1640 plays. See P 142, notes.

207 - Bussy D'Ambois. A. N. for R. Lunne, 1641. 4°. (G 246bI) CSmH, CtY, DFo, ICN, MH, NjP, TxU.

208 - - [Anr.issue.] 1641. 4°. (G 246bII) CSmH.

209 - - [Anr.issue.] T.W. for R.Lunne,1646. 4°. (G 246bIII) CSmH, DFo, MH.

210 - - [Anr.edn.] J. Kirton, 1657. 4°. (G 246bIV) British Museum, Dyce Collection.

   - - [Anr.edn.] 1691. See Durfey, T.

211 - Caesar and Pompey. Printed in the yeer 1652. 4°. MH, TxU.

212 - - [Anr.edn. or issue.] Printed in the yeare 1653. 4°. British Museum, Dyce Collection.

213 - Revenge for honour. Printed in the yeer 1654. 4°. (P 158) CtY, DFo, DLC, ICN, MH.

214 - - [Anr.issue.] R.Marriot, 1654. 4°. CSmH, DFo, MH. See P 158, notes.

215 - - [Anr.issue.] H. Moseley, 1659. 4°. CSmH, DFo. See P 158, notes.

216 - The tragedy of Alphonsus emperour of Germany. H. Moseley, 1654. 4°. CLUC, CSmH, CtY, DFo, DLC, MH, MWiW-C, NN, TxU.

CHARLES I. See *The famous tragedie of King Charles I.*

217 THE CHRISTMAS ORDINARY. J. Courtney, 1682. 4°.
CSmH, DFo, DLC, ICU, MH, NIC.

218 CIBBER, COLLEY
Love's last shift; or, The fool in fashion. H. Rhodes, R. Parker, and S. Briscoe, 1696. 4°. CLUC, CSmH, CtY, DFo, DLC, ICN, ICU, MH, MiU, NIC, NjP, PU, TxU.

219 - The tragical history of King Richard III. B. Lintott and A. Bettesworth, [1700.] 4°. CSmH, DFo, MH, MiU, NjP, TxU.

220 - Womans wit; or, The lady in fashion. J. Sturton, 1697. 4°. CSmH, CtY, DFo, ICN, ICU, MH, MiU, NjP.

221 - Xerxes. J. Nutt, 1699. 4°. CSmH, DFo, ICN, ICU, MH, TxU.

222 - - [Anr.issue.] R. Basset, 1699. 4°. CSmH.

223 - - [Anr.issue.] J. Nutt for R. Basset, 1699. 4°. CtY.

CICERO, MARCUS TULLIUS. See *The tragedy of that famous Roman oratour, Marcus Tullius Cicero.* 1650.

224 CLARK, WILLIAM
Marciano; or, The discovery. Edinburgh: Printed in the year, 1663. 4°. CSmH, DLC.

COCKAINE, SIR ASTON. See Cokayne, Sir A.

COCKBURN, CATHERINE. See Trotter, Catherine.

225 CODRINGTON, ROBERT
Ignoramus. W. Gilbertson, 1662. 4°. CSmH, CtY, DFo, MiU, TxU.
Translated from George Ruggle.

Small poems of divers sorts. W. Godbid, 1658. 8°. CLUC,
CSmH, DFo, DLC, TxU.

Contains *The obstinate lady* and *Trappolin creduto principe.*
Or Trappolin suppos'd a prince, with separate title-pages,
and *A masque presented at Bretbie in Darbyshire on
Twelfth-night.* 1639.

227 - - [Anr.issue, with cancel title-page.] A chain of golden poems
...together with...The obstinate lady, and Trappolin suppos'd a prince. W.G. and sold by I.Pridmore, 1658. 8°.
CSmH, CtY, DFo, MH.

228 - - [Anr.issue, with cancel title-page.] Poems. With The obstinate lady and Trapolin a supposed prince—Whereunto is
now added The tragedy of Ovid. P.Stephens jr.,1662. 8°.
CtY (The tragedy of Ovid only), DFo (The tragedy of Ovid
only), British Museum, Dyce Collection.

The tragedy of Ovid has independent title-page and is
signed A⁶, B-K⁸.

228a - - [Anr.issue.] F. Kirkman, 1662. [Hazlitt 1,93]

229 - - [Anr.issue, with cancel title-page.] Choice poems of several
sorts. With The obstinate lady, Trappolin, suppos'd a prince.
The tragedie of Ovid. F. Kirkman, 1669. 8°. CSmH, CtY,
DLC, ICN, MH.

The tragedie of Ovid is a different edition, signed A⁴, B-I⁸,
K⁶. [Hazlitt I,93 and Greg]

- A masque presented at Bretbie in Darbyshire on Twelfth-night.
1639. 1658. See his *Small poems,* 1658.

230 - The obstinate lady. W. Godbid for I. Pridmore, 1657. 4°.
CLUC, CSmH, CtY, DFo, DLC, ICU, MH, MWiW-C,
MiU.

- - [Anr.edn.] W. Godbid, 1658. See his *Small poems,* 1658.

- The tragedy of Ovid. See his *Poems,* 1662.

COKAYNE, SIR ASTON (continued)
Trappolin creduto principe. Or Trappolin suppos'd a prince.
W. Godbid, 1658. See his *Small poems*, 1658.

- - [Anr.edn.] See Tate, N., *A duke and no duke.*

A COMEDY CALLED THE MARRIAGE BROAKER; or,
The pander. 1662. In *Gratiae theatrales.* 1662.

231 CONGREVE, WILLIAM
The double-dealer. J. Tonson, 1694. 4°. (P 194; M 31)
CLUC, CSmH, CtY, DFo, DLC, ICN, ICU, MH, MWiW-C,
MiU, NjP, PU, TxU.

232 - Love for love. J. Tonson, 1695. 4°. (P 202) CSmH, CtY,
DLC, IEN, MH, MWiW-C, *MiU, TxU.
Signed A⁴, a⁴, B-M⁴, N².

233 - - [Anr.edn.] 1695. 4°. CSmH, CtY, DFo, ICU, MH, TxU.
Signed A-M⁴.

234 - - [Anr.edn.] 1695. 4°. CLUC, CSmH, CtY, ICN, MH, TxU.
Signed A-I⁴.

235 - - [Anr.edn.] 1695. 4°. (P 203) TxU.
Signed A-H⁴.

236 - - [Anr.edn.] 1697. 4°. CtY, DFo, ICU, MH, NjP.

237 - The mourning bride. J. Tonson, 1697. 4°. (P 205) CLUC,
CSmH, CtY, DFo, DLC, ICN, ICU, MH, MWiW-C, MiU,
NjP, PU, TxU.

238 - - [Anr.edn.] 1697. 4°. CLUC, DFo, MH, NjP, TxU.
"Second edition."

239 - - [Anr.edn.] 1679 [i.e. 1697.] 4°. (P 206) CtY, MH, NjP.
"Second edition."

CONGREVE, WILLIAM (continued)

240   The old batchelour. P. Buck, 1693. 4°. (P 208) CLUC, CSmH, CtY, DFo, DLC, ICN, MH, MWiW-C, NN, TxU.

241 - - [Anr.edn.] 1693. 4°. CtY, DFo, MH, TxU.
"Second" edition. This and the following two editions are really re-issues of the first edition with some pages re-set.

242 - - [Anr.edn.] 1693. 4°. CtY, MH, TxU.
"Third" edition.

243 - - [Anr.edn.] 1693. 4°. CtY, DFo, MH.
"Fourth" edition.

244 - - [Anr.edn.] To be sold by all booksellers, 1693. 4°. CSmH.

245 - - [Anr.edn.] P. Buck, sold by J. Knapton, 1694. 4°. CSmH.

246 - - [Anr.issue.] P. Buck, 1694. 4°. CtY, MH, TxU.

247 - - [Anr.issue.] J. Knapton, 1694. 4°. DFo, MH.

248 - - [Anr.edn.] P. Buck, 1697. 4°. CtY, DFo, ICU, MH, NIC, TxU.

249 - The way of the world. J. Tonson, 1700. 4°. CLUC, CSmH, CtY, DFo, DLC, MH, MWiW-C, TxU.

250 THE CONSTANT NYMPH; or, The rambling shepheard. L. Curtis, 1678. 4°. CLUC, CSmH, CtY, DFo, DLC, ICN, ICU, MH, MiU.
CSmH also reports a variant copy with different setting of type on Sheet E.

251 THE CONVERTED FRYAR; or, A defiance to the Church of Rome. By W. P. H. B., 1673. 4°. CSmH.

252 COOKE, EDWARD
Love's triumph; or, The royal union. T. James, sold by him

and W. Leach, 1678. 4°. CSmH, CtY, DFo, DLC, ICN, ICU, MH, MiU, TxU.

CORNEILLE, PIERRE
The Cid. See Rutter, J.

- Heraclius. See Carlell, L.

- Horace. 1671. See Cotton, C.

- Horace. 1667, 1669, 1678. See Philips, K.

- Horatius, a Roman tragedie. 1656. See Lower, Sir W.

- The mistaken beauty. See under title.

- Nicomede. See Dancer, J.

- Polyeuctes. See Lower, Sir W.

- Pompey. See Philips, K.

- Pompey the great. See Waller, E.

CORNEILLE, THOMAS
Amorous Orontus. 1665. See Bulteel, J.

- - [Anr.edn. with changed title.] The amorous gallant. 1675. See Bulteel, J.

- Dame Dobson. 1684. See Ravenscroft, E.

- The extravagant sheepherd. 1654. See under title.

- The feign'd astrologer. 1668. See under title.

253 THE CORNISH COMEDY. D. Brown, T. Bennet, and K. Gately, 1696. 4°. CLUC, CSmH, CtY, DFo, DLC, ICN, ICU, MH, MiU, NN, TxU.

254 THE CORONATION OF QUEEN ELIZABETH, with the
     restauration of the Protestant religion. B. Harris, 1680. 4°.
     CSmH, ICU.

255 CORYE, JOHN
     The generous enemies; or, The ridiculous lovers. H. Lloyd for
     J. Magnus, 1672. 4°. CSmH, CtY, DFo, DLC, ICN, ICU,
     MH, MWiW-C, MiU, NjP, TxU.

256 COTTON, CHARLES
     Horace. H. Brome, 1671. 4°. CLUC, CSmH, CtY, DFo,
     ICU, MWiW-C, NN, TxU.
     Translated from P. Corneille.

THE COUNTERFEIT BRIDEGROOM. 1677. See Behn, A.

257 Entry cancelled.

COWLEY, ABRAHAM
Cutter of Coleman-street. See No. 260.

258 - The guardian. J. Holden, 1650. 4°. DFo.
     The verso of the title-page is blank.

259 - - [Anr. issue with cancel title-page, the verso of which bears
     "The Actors Names."] J. Holden, 1650. 4°. (P 225) CSmH,
     CtY, DFo, DLC, ICU, MH, MWiW-C.

260 - - [Anr. edn. revised, with changed title.] Cutter of Coleman-
     street. H. Herringman, 1663. 4°. (P 226) CSmH, CtY,
     DFo, DLC, IEN, MH, MWiW-C, NN, NjP, TxU.

261 - - [Anr. edn.] H. Herringman, sold by R. Bentley, J. Tonson,
     F. Saunders, and T. Bennet, 1693. fol. In his *Works,* 1693,
     or separate. CLUC, DFo, DLC, ICN, ICU, IEN, MH, MiU,
     TxU.

262 - - [Anr.edn.] 1700. fol. In his *Works,* H. Herringman, sold by J. Tonson and T. Bennet, 1700. CLUC, CSmH, CtY, DFo, DLC, IEN, MH, NN, NjP.

263 - Loves riddle. M. D. for C. Harper and J. Tonson, 1681. fol. In his *The second part of the works,* 1681. CLUC, CtY, DFo, DLC, ICU, MH, MiU, NN, TxU.

264 - - [Anr.edn.] M. Clark for C. Harper and J. Tonson, 1682. 12 mo. In his *The second part of the works,* 1682. CLUC, CSmH, DFo, ICU, MH, NN, PU.

265 - - [Anr.edn.] M. C. for C. Harper and A. Swalle, 1684. fol. In his *The second part of the works,* 1684. DFo, MH, PU, TxU.

266 - - [Anr.edn.] M. Clark for C. Harper, 1687. fol. In his *The second and third parts of the works.* C. Harper, 1689. *CLUC, DFo, *DLC, ICN, *ICU, *MH, *MiU, *TxU.

267 - - [Anr.issue.] In his *The second and third parts of the works.* C. Harper, 1689. DFo.
After line 12 of the general title-page are the words, "Never before published in English."

268 - - [Anr.edn.] M. Clark for C. Harper, 1700. fol. In his *The second and third parts of the works.* C. Harper, 1700. CLUC. CSmH, CtY, DFo, MH, NN, NjP.

269 - Naufragium joculare. Typis M. C.; veneunt apud C. Harper, & J. Tonson, 1681. fol. In his *The second part of the works,* M. Clark for C. Harper and J. Tonson, 1681. CLUC, CtY, DFo, DLC, ICU, MH, MiU, NN, TxU.

270 - - [Anr.edn.] Typis M. C.; veneunt apud C. Harper, & J. Tonson, 1682. 12 mo. In his *The second part of the works,* M. Clark for C. Harper and J. Tonson, 1682. CLUC, CSmH, DFo, ICU, MH, NN, PU.

31

COWLEY, ABRAHAM (continued)

271 - - [Anr.edn.] Typis M. Clark; veneunt apud C. Harper and A. Swalle, 1684. fol. In his *The second part of the works*. M. C. for C. Harper and A. Swalle, 1684. DFo, MH, PU, TxU.

272 - - [Anr.edn.] Typis M. Clark; veneunt apud C. Harper, 1687. fol. In his *The second and third parts of the works*. C. Harper, 1689. *CLUC, DFo, *DLC, ICN, *ICU, *MH, *MiU, *TxU.

273 - - [Anr.issue.] In his *The second and third parts of the works*. C. Harper, 1689. DFo.
　　　After line 12 of the general title-page are the words, "Never before published in English."

274 - - [Anr.edn.] Typis M. Clark; veneunt apud C. Harper, 1700. fol. In his *The second and third parts of the works*. C. Harper, 1700. CLUC, CSmH, CtY, DFo, MH, NN, NjP.

275 COX, ROBERT
　　　Actaeon and Diana. T. Newcomb for the use of the author, n. d. 4°. CSmH, DFo, MH, MWiW-C.

276 - - [Anr.edn.] E. Archer, 1656. 4°. CSmH.

　　- Singing Simpkin. 1656. In his *Actaeon and Diana*.

　　- The wits. 1662. See *The wits; or, Sport upon sport*. Part I.

277 CROWNE, JOHN
　　　The ambitious statesman; or, The loyal favourite. W. Abington, 1679. 4°. CLUC, CSmH, CtY, DFo, DLC, ICN, ICU, MH, MWiW-C, MiU, NIC, NN, NjP.

278 - - [Anr.edn.] R. Bentley and M. Magnes, 1681 4°. CtY, MH.

279 - Andromache. T. Ratcliffe and N. Thompson for R. Bentley, 1675. 4°. CLUC, CSmH, DFo, DLC, ICN, ICU, MH, MWiW-C, NN, NjP, TxU.
　　　Translated from Racine.

CROWNE, JOHN (continued)

280   Caligula. J. Orme for R. Wellington, sold by P. Gilborne and B. Lintott, 1698. 4°. CLUC, CSmH, CtY, DFo, DLC, ICN, ICU, MH, MWiW-C, NN, NjP, TxU.

281 - Calisto; or, The chaste nimph. T. Newcomb for J. Magnes and R. Bentley, 1675. 4°. CLUC, CSmH, CtY, DFo, DLC, ICN, ICU, MH, MWiW-C, MiU, NN, NjP, TxU.

282 - City politiques. R. Bently and J. Hindmarsh, 1683. 4°. CLUC, CSmH (2 variant copies), CtY, DFo, DLC, ICN, MH, MWiW-C, NN, NjP, TxU.

283 - - [Anr.edn.] R. Bently and J. Hindmarsh, 1688. 4°. CSmH, CtY, DFo, DLC, ICN, ICU, MH, MiU, TxU.

284 - The countrey wit. T. N. for J. Magnes and R. Bentley, 1675. 4°. CLUC, CSmH, CtY, DFo, DLC, ICN, ICU, MH, MWiW-C, NN, TxU.

285 - - [Anr.edn.] T. Chapman, 1693. 4°. CtY, DFo, DLC, ICU, MH, MiU, NjP.

286 - Darius King of Persia. R. Bentley, 1688. 4°. CSmH, DFo, DLC, ICN, ICU, MH, MWiW-C, NN, NjP, TxU.

287 - - [Anr.issue.] J. Knight and F. Saunders, 1688. 4°. CLUC, CSmH, CtY, DFo, MH, MWiW-C, MiU, NjP, TxU.

288 - The destruction of Jerusalem by Titus Vespasian. In two parts. J. Magnes and R. Bentley, 1677. 4°. CLUC, CSmH, CtY, DFo, DLC, ICN, ICU, MH, NIC, NN, NjP, TxU.

289 - - [Anr.edn.] R. Bentley, 1693. 4°. CtY, DFo, MH, MiU.

290 - The English frier; or, The town sparks. J. Knapton, 1690. 4°. CLUC, CSmH, CtY, DFo, DLC, ICN, ICU, MH, MWiW-C, MiU, NIC, NN, NjP, TxU.

CROWNE, JOHN (continued)

291   Henry the sixth, the first part. With the murder of Humphrey Duke of Glocester. [The second part; or, The misery of civil war] R. Bentley and M. Magnes, 1681. 4°. (P 912) CLUC (2nd part), CSmH, CtY, DFo, DLC, ICN, ICU, MH, MWiW-C, MiU (1st part), NN (1st part), PU (2nd part), TxU.

    The second part was first published in 1680 as *The misery of civil war*. See no. 296.

292 - The history of Charles the eighth of France; or, The invasion of Naples by the French. T. R. and N. T. for A. Isted, 1672. 4°. CLUC, CSmH, CtY, DFo, DLC, ICN, ICU, MH, MWiW-C, MiU, NIC, NN, NjP, TxU.

293 - - [Anr.issue.] A. I., sold by R. Boulter, 1680. 4°. DLC, MH.

294 - Juliana; or, The princess of Poland. W. Cademan and W. Birch, 1671. 4°. CLUC, CSmH, (2 variant copies), CtY, DFo, DLC, ICU, MH, MWiW-C, MiU, NN.

295 - The married beau; or, The curious impertinent. R. Bentley, 1694. 4°. CLUC, CSmH, CtY, DFo, DLC, ICN, ICU, MH, MWiW-C, MiU, NIC, NN, NjP, PU, TxU.

296 - The misery of civil-war. R. Bentley and M. Magnes, 1680. 4°. (P 913) CLUC, CSmH, CtY, DFo, DLC, ICN, ICU, MH, NN, NjP, PU.

    Reissued in 1681 as the second part of *Henry the sixth*. See no. 291.

297 - The prologue to Calistho, with the chorus's between the acts. Printed in the year 1675. 4°. DFo.

298 - Regulus. J. Knapton, 1694. 4°. CLUC, CSmH, CtY, DFo, DLC, ICU, MH, MWiW-C, MiU, NN, NjP, TxU.

299 - Sir Courtly Nice; or, It cannot be. H. H. jun. for R. Bently and J. Hindmarsh, 1685. 4°. CLUC, CSmH, CtY, DFo, DLC, ICN, ICU, MH, MWiW-C, MiU, NIC, NN, NjP, TxU.

CROWNE, JOHN (continued)
300 - - [Anr.edn.] M.B. for R.Bentley, 1693. 4°. CtY, DLC, MH.

301 - - [Anr.issue.] M. B. for R. Bently and J. Hindmarsh, 1693. 4°. DFo.

302 - Thyestes. R. Bently and M. Magnes, 1681. 4°. CLUC, CSmH, CtY, DFo, DLC, ICN, ICU, MH, MWiW-C, NIC, NN, NjP, TxU.

303 DABORNE, ROBERT
The poor-mans comfort. R. Pollard and J. Sweeting, 1655. 4°. CLUC, CSmH, DFo, DLC, ICN, ICU, MH, PU.

304 DANCER, JOHN
Agrippa king of Alba; or, The false Tiberinus. J.C. for N. Cox, 1675. 4°. CSmH, DFo, DLC, MH, NjP.
Translated from P. Quinault.

305 - Aminta: the famous pastoral. J. Starkey, 1660. 8°. CSmH, CtY, MiU, PU.
Translated from T. Tasso.

306 - Nicomede. F. Kirkman, 1671. 4°. CLUC, CSmH, CtY, DFo, DLC, ICU, MH, MiU, NIC, TxU.
Translated from P. Corneille.

307 DAVENANT, CHARLES
Circe. R. Tonson, 1677. 4°. CLUC, CSmH, CtY, DFo, DLC, ICN, ICU, MH, MWiW-C, NIC, NN, NjP, TxU.

308 - - The second edn. R. Tonson, 1685. 4°. CtY, DFo, ICN, NjP, TxU.

309 DAVENANT, SIR WILLIAM
The works. T. N. for H. Herringman, 1673. fol. CLUC, CSmH, CtY, DFo, DLC, ICN, ICU, IEN, MH, MWiW-C, MiU, NIC, NN, NjP, PU, TxU.

310   Two excellent plays: The wits, a comedie. The platonick lovers, a tragi-comedie. G. Bedel and T. Collins, 1665. 8°.
    (P 262) CSmH, CtY, DFo, DLC, ICU, MH, NjP.

311 - The cruelty of the Spaniards in Peru. H. Herringman, 1658.
    4°. (P 251) CLUC, CSmH, CtY, DFo, DLC, MH,
    MWiW-C, NN.

312 - The first days entertainment at Rutland-House. J.M. for H.
    Herringman, 1657. 8°. CSmH, CtY, DFo, MH, MWiW-C,
    TxU.

    - Hamlet. See his *The tragedy of Hamlet prince of Denmark.*

313 - The history of Sir Francis Drake. Part I. H. Herringman,
    1659. 4°. (P 255) CSmH, CtY, ICN, MH, MWiW-C,
    NN.

314 - Love and honour. H. Robinson and H. Moseley, 1649. 4°.
    (P 257) CSmH, CtY, DFo, DLC, ICN, MH, MWiW-C,
    PU, TxU.

315 - Macbeth. P. Chetwin, 1674. 4°. CLUC, CSmH, CtY, DFo,
    DLC, MH, NN, PU.

316 - - [Anr.edn.] A. Clark, 1674. 4°. DFo, MH, MiU, PU.

317 - - [Anr.edn.] H. Herringman, sold by J. Knight and F. Saunders, 1687. 4°. (P 914) CSmH, DFo, MiU, PU, TxU.

318 - - [Anr.issue.] H. Herringman and R. Bentley, sold by T.
    Chapman, 1687. 4°. DFo, MH.

319 - - [Anr.edn.] H. Herringman and R. Bentley, sold by R. Bentley, J. Tonson, T. Bennet and F. Sanders, 1695. 4°. CLUC,
    CSmH, DFo, ICN, MH.

320 - - [Anr.edn.] 1697. (CBEL, I, 454)

321 The man's the master. H. Herringman, 1669. 4°. (P 259)
CLUC, CSmH, CtY, DFo, DLC, ICN, ICU, MII, MWiW-C,
TxU.

- The platonick lovers. 1655. In his *Two excellent plays.*

322 - The rivals. W. Cademan, 1668. 4°. CLUC, CSmH, CtY,
DFo, ICN, MH, MWiW-C, NN, NjP.

323 - - [Anr.issue.] 1669. 4°. DFo.

324 - The siege of Rhodes. J. M. for H. Herringman, 1656. 4°.
CSmH, CtY, ICN, ICU, TxU.

325 - - [Anr.edn.] J. M. for H. Herringman, 1659. 4°. CSmH,
CtY, MH.

326 - - [Anr.edn.] The first and second part. H. Herringman,
1663. 4°. CLUC, CSmH, CtY, DFo (Part II), ICU, MH,
NjP (Part II), TxU.

327 - - [Anr.edn.] H. Herringman, 1670. 4°. CSmH, CtY, DFo,
DLC, ICN, ICU, MH, NN, NjP, TxU.

328 - The tempest; or, The enchanted island. J. M. for H. Herring-
man, 1670. 4°. (M 73a) CLUC, CSmH, DFo, DLC, *PU,
*TxU.
Page seven incorrectly numbered.

329 - - [Anr.issue.] (M 73a) CLUC, CSmH, CtY, DFo, MH,
MWiW-C, MiU, NIC.
Pagination corrected.

330 - - [Anr.edn.] T. N. for H. Herringman, 1674. 4°. (M 73b)
CLUC, CSmH, DFo, MH, PU, TxU.
This and the following editions have some additions and
alterations by Thomas Shadwell.

DAVENANT, SIR WILLIAM (continued)

331 - - [Anr.edn.] J. Macock for H. Herringman, 1676. 4°. (M 73c)
    CLUC, CSmH, CtY, DFo, MH, NN, *PU, TxU.
        Signed A-L⁴, M².

332 - - [Anr.edn.] 1676. 4°. (M 73e) DFo, ICN, MH, TxU.
        "Priented" in imprint. Probably printed about 1692 in-
        stead of 1676.

333 - - [Anr.edn.] 1676. 4°. DFo.
        Signed A⁸, B-I⁴, K¹.

334 - - [Anr.edn.] J. M. for H. Herringman, sold by R. Bentley,
        1690. 4°. (M 73d) CLUC, CSmH, CtY, DFo, DLC, ICU,
        MH, MiU, NN, NjP, PU, TxU.

335 - - [Anr.edn.] T. Warren for H. Herringman, sold by R. Bent-
        ley, J. Tonson, F. Saunders, and T. Bennet, 1695. 4°.
        (M 73f) CLUC, CSmH, DFo, MH, MiU, NIC, NN, PU,
        TxU.

336 - The tragedy of Hamlet prince of Denmark. A. Clark for J.
        Martyn and H. Herringman, 1676. 4°. (G 197i) CSmH,
        CtY, DFo, MH.
        4-line imprint.

337 - - [Anr.edn.] 1676. 4°. (G 197j) CLUC, CSmH, DFo,
        MiU.
        5-line imprint.

338 - - [Anr.edn.] H.Heringman and R.Bentley, 1683. 4°.
        (G 197k) CLUC, CSmH, CtY, DFo, MH, PU, TxU.
        DFo has also an early state of the imprint, with the read-
        ing "Heringham."

339 - - [Anr.edn.] R. Bentley, J. Tonson, T. Bennet, and F. Saun-
        ders, 1695. 4°. MH.

340 - - [Anr.issue.]   H. Herringman and R. Bentley, sold by R.
Bentley, J. Tonson, T. Bennet, and F. Sanders, 1695.   4°.
(G 197m*)   DFo, MH, PU.

341 - - [Anr.issue.]   R. Bentley, 1695.   4°.   (G 197m+) DFo, MH.

342 - The unfortunate lovers.   R. H., sold by F. Coles, 1643.   4°.
CLUC, CSmH, CtY, DFo, MH.

343 - - [Anr.edn.]   H. Moseley, 1649.   4°.   CLUC, CSmH, MH.

- The wits.   1665.   In his *Two excellent plays.*

344 DAVENPORT, ROBERT
The city-night-cap; or, Crede quod habes & habes.   J. Cottrel
for S. Speed, 1661.   4°.   CSmH (2 variant copies), CtY,
DFo, DLC, ICN, ICU, MH, MWiW-C, NjP, TxU.

345 - King John and Matilda.   A. Pennycuicke, 1655.   4°.   (P 263)
CLUC, CSmH, CtY, DFo, DLC, ICN, ICU, MH, MWiW-C.

346 - - [Anr.edn.]   R. Gammon, 1662.   4°.   DFo, ICN.

347 DAY, JOHN
The blind-beggar of Bednal-Green, with The merry humor of
Tom Strowd the Norfolk yeoman.   R. Pollard and T. Dring,
1659.   4°.   CSmH, CtY, DFo, ICN, MH, MWiW-C, NN,
TxU.

- Lusts dominion. See Marlowe, C.

348 - The parliament of bees.   W. Lee, 1641.   4°.   CSmH, DFo,
MH.

DEKKER, THOMAS
Lusts dominion.   See Marlowe, C.

349 - The shoomakers holiday.   W. Gilbertson, 1657.   4°.   (G 175f)
DLC.

DEKKER, THOMAS (continued)
The sun's-darling. See Ford, J. and T. Dekker.

- The virgin martyr. 1651. See Massinger, P. and T. Dekker.

- The witch of Edmonton. 1658. See Rowley, W., T. Dekker, and J. Ford.

DENHAM, SIR JOHN
Horace. See Philips, Katherine.

350 - The sophy. R. Hearne for T. Walkley, 1642. fol. (P 286)
CLUC, CSmH, DFo, CtY, ICU, MH, TxU.

351 - - [Anr. edn.] J. M. for H. Herringman, 1667. 8°. In his
Poems and translations, with The sophy. H. Herringman,
1668 (P 285) CLUC, CSmH, CtY, DFo, DLC, ICU, MH,
MWiW-C, NjP, TxU.

352 - - [Anr. edn.] 1671. 8°. In his *Poems and translations, with
The sophy.* J. M. for H. Herringman, 1671. CSmH, CtY,
DFo, DLC, ICU, MH, MiU, PU.

353 - - [Anr. edn.] 1684. 8°. In his *Poems and translations, with
The sophy.* J. M. for H. Herringman; and sold by J. Knight
and F. Saunders, 1684. CSmH, CtY, DFo, ICU, IEN, MH,
NIC, NjP.

354 DENNIS, JOHN
Iphigenia. R. Parker, 1700. 4°. CSmH, CtY, DFo, DLC,
ICN, ICU, MH, MiU, NjP, TxU.

355 - A plot and no plot. R. Parker, P. Buck, and R. Wellington,
[1697.] 4°. (P 288) CLUC, CSmH, CtY, DFo, DLC,
ICN, ICU, MH, MWiW-C, MiU, NjP, PU, TxU.

356 - Rinaldo and Armida. J. Tonson, 1699. 4°. CLUC, CSmH,
CtY, DFo, DLC, ICN, ICU, MH, MiU, NjP, TxU.

357 DIGBY, GEORGE, Earl of Bristol
   Elvira; or, The worst not always true. E. Cotes for H. Broom,
   1667. 4°. CLUC, CSmH, CtY, DFo, DLC, ICN, ICU,
   IEN, TxU.
   Imprint of Folger copy reads "Brome."

358 - - [Anr.edn.] A. C. for H. Brome, 1677. 4°. CSmH.

359 - - [Anr.edn.] 1685. (CBEL, II, 418).

360 DILKE, THOMAS
   The city lady; or, Folly reclaim'd. H. Newman, 1697. 4°
   CLUC, CSmH, CtY, DFo, DLC, ICU, MWiW-C, MiU,
   TxU

361 - The lover's luck. H. Playford and B. Tooke, 1696. 4°. (P 290)
   CSmH, CtY, DFo, DLC, ICN, ICU, MH, MiU, NjP, TxU.

362 - - [Anr.issue.] H. Newman, 1696. 4°. MWiW-C.

363 - The pretenders; or, The town unmaskt. P. Buck, 1698. 4°.
   (P 291) CSmH, CtY, DFo, DLC, ICN, ICU, MH,
   MWiW-C, MiU, NjP, PU.

364 DOGGETT, THOMAS
   The country-wake. S. Briscoe, sold by R. Wellington and R.
   Parker, 1696. 4°. CLUC, CSmH, CtY, DFo, DLC, ICN,
   ICU, MH, MiU, NIC, NjP, TxU.

365 - - [Anr.edn.] S. Briscoe, sold by R. Wellington and R. Parker, [1697.] 4°. CSmH, DFo, ICU, MH, TxU.

366 D'OUVILLY, GEORGE GERBIER
   The false favourit disgrac'd; and the reward of loyalty. W.
   Wilson for R. Crofts, 1657. 8°. CSmH, DFo, *MH.

367 - - [Anr.issue.] R. Crofts, 1657. 8°. CtY, DFo, NN.

DOVER, JOHN
The mall. See under title.

DOVER, JOHN (continued)

368   The Roman generalls; or, The distressed ladies.   S. Herrick,
      1667. 4°. CLUC, CSmH, CtY, DFo, DLC, ICN, ICU,
      MiU, TxU.

369 DRAKE, JAMES

      The sham-lawyer; or, The lucky extravagant. A. Roper, 1697.
      4°. CSmH, DFo, DLC.

370 DRYDEN, JOHN

      The works of Mr. John Dryden. [35 pieces set out in double
      column separated by a double bracket.] J. Tonson, 1691. 4°.
      (M 106a) Worcester College.
          A title-leaf printed for insertion in the first volume of a
      nonce collection of the plays and poems.

371 - The works of Mr. John Dryden in four volumes... [the con-
      tents of the four volumes in double column]. J. Tonson,
      1693. 4°. (M 106b) CLUC, DFo (III and IV only).
          Title-leaves printed for insertion in nonce collections of
      the plays, poems, etc.

372 - The works... In four volumes. J. Tonson, 1694. 4°. (M 106c)
      DFo, MH.
          Not a general title-page but a leaf of advertisement printed
      on the verso of the half-title of *Love triumphant* and in-
      serted in the first volume of a nonce collection. In one set,
      the second volume had no general title; in volumes three
      and four were title-pages dated 1695, i.e. M 106e.

373 - Mr. Dryden's plays. In two volumes. Vol. I. Tragedies. Es-
      say on dramatic poesie [and 15 plays in alphabetical order].
      T. Warren for H. Herringman, sold by R. Bentley, J. Ton-
      son, F. Saunders, and T. Bennet, 1694. 4°. (M 106d) DFo.
          This title is printed on leaf L2r of Porter's *The villain*,
      1694. No copy of the title of volume two has been traced.

374 - The first... The second... The third... The fourth volume
      of the works of Mr. John Dryden... J. Tonson, 1695. 4°.
      (M 106e) CLUC, CtY (lacks III), DFo.
          Title-leaves printed for insertion in nonce collections.

375 The dramatick works of Mr. John Dryden. In three volumes.
R. Bentley, 1695. 4°. (M 106f) CLUC, DFo, MH (I only).
Title-leaves printed for insertion in nonce collections.

376 - Albion and Albanius. J. Tonson, 1685. fol. (M 88a ;P 312)
CLUC, CSmH, CtY, DFo, DLC, ICU, MH, MWiW-C, TxU.
CSmH, DFo and TxU have also the variant copies de-
scribed in M 88a.

376a- - [Anr.issue.] 1685. fol. CSmH, DFo, TxU.
With an unsigned leaf with prologue and epilogue.

377 - - [Anr.edn.] For the author, sold by W. Nott, 1687. fol.
(M 88b) CLUC, CSmH, MH.

378 - - [Anr.edn.] J. Tonson, 1691. 4°. (M 88c) CLUC, CSmH,
CtY, DFo, ICN, ICU, MH, MiU, NIC, NjP, TxU.

379 - All for love; or, The world well lost. T. Newcomb for H.
Herringman, 1678. 4°. (M 82a ;P 313) CLUC, CSmH,
CtY, DFo, DLC, ICN, ICU, MH, MWiW-C, MiU, NIC,
NjP, PU, TxU.

380 - - [Anr.edn.] H. Herringman, sold by R. Bently, J. Tonson,
F. Saunders, and T. Bennet, 1692. 4°. (M 82b) CLUC,
CSmH, CtY, DFo, ICU, MH, MiU, PU, TxU.

381 - - [Anr.edn.] T. Warren for H. Herringman, sold by R. Bent-
ley, J. Tonson, F. Saunders, and T. Bennet, 1696. 4°. (M 82c)
CLUC, CSmH, CtY, DFo, ICN, ICU, MH, MiU, NjP, PU,
TxU.

- Almanzor and Almahide; or, The conquest of Granada, The
second part. See his *The conquest of Granada.*

382 - Amboyna. T. N. for H. Herringman, 1673. 4°. (M 79a ;
P 314) CLUC, CSmH, CtY, DFo, DLC, ICN, ICU, MH,
MWiW-C, MiU, NjP, TxU.
DFO has all, and TxU has two, of the three states of a2ᵛ
described in M 79a.

DRYDEN, JOHN (continued)

383 - - [Anr.issue.]   1673.   4°.   (M 79a; P 314)   CSmH, MH,
TxU.
    Printer's ornaments on t.-p.

384 - - [Anr.edn.]   H. Herringman, sold by R. Bentley, 1691.   4°.
(M 79b)   CLUC, CSmH, CtY, DFo, DLC, ICN, IEN, MH,
MiU, NjP, TxU.

385 - Amphitryon; or, The two Socia's.   J. Tonson and M. Tonson,
1690.   4°.   (M 90ai)   CLUC, CSmH, CtY, DFo, MH.

386 - - [Anr.issue.]   1691.   4°.   (M 90aii; P 315)   CLUC, CSmH,
CtY, DFo, DLC, ICN, ICU, MH, TxU.

387 - - [Anr.edn.]   J. Tonson, 1694.   4°.   (M 90b)   CLUC, CtY,
DFo, DLC, ICN, ICU, MH, MiU, NIC, NN, NjP, TxU.

388 - The assignation; or, Love in a nunnery.   T. N. for H. Herringman, 1673.   4°.   (M 78a; P 318)   CLUC, CSmH, CtY, DFo,
DLC, ICN, MH, MWiW-C, MiU, TxU.
    TxU has two variant copies, differing only in head-piece
over dedication.

389 - - [Anr.edn.]   1678.   4°.   (M 78b)   CLUC, CSmH, CtY,
DFo, DLC, ICN, ICU, MH, MiU, NjP, TxU.

390 - - [Anr.edn.]   R. Bently, J. Tonson, F. Saunders, and T. Bennet, 1692.   4°.   (M 78c)   CLUC, CSmH, CtY, DFo, DLC,
ICN, ICU, MH, MiU, NN, NjP, TxU.

391 - Aureng-Zebe.   T. N. for H. Herringman, 1676.   4°.   (M 80a;
P 319)   CLUC, CSmH, CtY, DFo, DLC, ICN, ICU, MH,
MWiW-C, MiU, NjP, NN, TxU.

392 - - [Anr.edn.]   J. M. for H. Herringman, sold by J. Knight
and F. Saunders, 1685.   4°.   (M 80b)   CLUC, CSmH, CtY,
DFo, ICU, MH, MiU, NIC, PU, TxU.

DRYDEN, JOHN (continued)

393 - - [Anr.edn.] H. Herringman, 1690. 4°. (M 80c) CLUC, CtY, DFo, MH.

394 - - [Anr.edn.] H. Herringman, sold by R. Bentley, J. Tonson, F. Saunders, and T. Bennet, 1692. 4°. (M 80d) CLUC, CtY, DFo, DLC, MH, TxU.

395 - - [Anr.edn.] 1694. 4°. (M 80e) CLUC, CSmH, CtY, DFo, ICN, ICU, MH, NN, NjP, TxU.

396 - - [Anr.edn.] T. Warren for H. Herringman, sold by J. Tonson, F. Saunders, and T. Bennet, 1699. 4°. (M 80f) CLUC, DFo, MH, NIC, TxU.

397 - Cleomenes, the Spartan hero. J. Tonson, 1692. 4°. (M 92; P 321) CLUC, CSmH, CtY, DFo, DLC, ICN, ICU, IEN, MH, MiU, NjP, TxU.

398 - The conquest of Granada by the Spaniards. 2 parts. T. N. for H. Herringman, 1672. 4°. (M 76a) CLUC, CSmH, CtY, DFo, DLC, ICU, MH, MWiW-C, NN, NjP, TxU.

399 - - [Anr.edn.] 1673. 4°. (M 76b) CLUC, CSmH, CtY, DFo, DLC, MH, TxU.

400 - - [Anr.edn.] H. Hills for H. Herringman, 1678. 4°. (M 76c) CLUC, CtY, DFo, ICU, MH, MiU, NN, TxU.

401 - - [Anr.edn.] J. M. for H. Herringman, sold by J. Knight and F. Saunders, 1687. 4°. (M 76d) CLUC, CtY, DFo, ICU, IEN, MH, MiU, NIC, NjP, PU, TxU.

402 - - [Anr.edn.] H. Herringman, sold by R. Bentley, J. Tonson, F. Saunders, and T. Bennet, 1695. 4°. (M 76e) CLUC, CtY, DFo, DLC, ICN, ICU, MH, TxU.

- Dialogue. 1700. See Vanbrugh, J. *The Pilgrim.*

DRYDEN, JOHN (continued)

403　Don Sebastian, King of Portugal.　J. Hindmarsh, 1690.　4°.
　　(M 89a; P 322)　CLUC, CSmH, CtY, DFo, DLC, ICN,
　　ICU, MH, MWiW-C, MiU, NIC, NjP, TxU.

404 - - [Anr.edn.]　1692.　4°.　(M 89b)　CLUC, CSmH, CtY,
　　DFo, ICN, ICU, MH, NIC, NjP, TxU.

405 - The Duke of Guise.　T. H. for R. Bentley and J. Tonson, 1683.
　　4°.　(M 87a; P 323)　CLUC, CSmH, CtY, DFo, DLC,
　　ICN, ICU, MH, MWiW-C, MiU, NjP, TxU.
　　In collaboration with N. Lee.

406 - - [Anr.edn.]　R. E. for R. Bentley and J. Tonson, 1687.　4°.
　　(M 87b)　CLUC, CSmH, CtY, DFo, ICN, IEN, MH, MiU,
　　NN, NjP, TxU.

407 - - [Anr.edn.]　J. Tonson, 1699.　4°.　(M 87c)　CtY, DFo,
　　ICU, MH, TxU.

408 - - [Anr.issue.]　R. Wellington and　E. Rombull, 1699.　4°.
　　(M 87d)　CLUC, CtY, DFo, MH, TxU.

409 - An evening's love; or, The mock-astrologer.　T. N. for H.
　　Herringman, 1671.　4°. (M 75a)　CLUC, CSmH, CtY, DFo
　　(2 variants), DLC, ICN, MH, TxU.
　　Signed A⁴, a⁴, b², A-L⁴, M²; 56 1.

410 - - [Anr.edn.]　1671.　4°.　(M 75b; P 325)　CLUC, CSmH,
　　CtY, DFo, ICN, ICU, MH, MWiW-C, MiU, NN, NjP,
　　TxU.
　　Signed A-N⁴, O²; 54 1.

411 - - [Anr.edn.]　1675.　4°.　(M 75c)　CLUC, CtY, DFo.

412 - - [Anr.issue.]　H. Herringman, 1675.　4°.　(M 75c)　MH.

DRYDEN, JOHN (continued)

413 - - [Anr.edn.] H. Herringman, sold by R. Bentley, 1691. 4°.
(M 75d) CLUC, CSmH, CtY, DFo, ICU, IEN, MH, MiU,
NjP, TxU.

414 - The Indian emperour ; or, The conquest of Mexico by the Spaniards. J. M. for H. Herringman, 1667. 4°. (M 69a) CLUC,
CSmH, CtY, DFo, MH, TxU.

415 - - [Anr.edn.] H. Herringman, 1668. 4° (M 69b) CSmH,
CtY, DFo, MH, TxU.
With "Defense of an essay of Dramatic Poesy."

416 - - [Anr.issue.] 1668. 4°. (M 69b) CLUC, CSmH, ICN,
MH, MiU, TxU.
Without "Defense of an essay of Dramatic Poesy."

417 - - [Anr.edn.] 1670. 4°. (M 69c) CLUC, *CSmH, DFo,
TxU.
"Emperour" in title.

418 - - [Anr.edn.] 1670. 4°. (M 69d) CLUC, CtY, DFo, ICN,
ICU, MH, NjP, TxU.
"Emperor" in title.

419 - - [Anr.edn.] 1681. 4°. (M 69e) CLUC, CSmH, CtY, DFo,
DLC, MH, MiU, NN, TxU.

420 - - [Anr.edn.] H. Herringman, sold by J. Knight and F. Saunders, 1686. 4°. (M 69f) CLUC, CSmH, CtY, DFo, ICN,
ICU, MH, MiU, TxU.

421 - - [Anr.edn.] H. Herringman, sold by R. Bentley, J. Tonson,
F. Saunders, and T. Bennet, 1692. 4°. (M 69g) CLUC,
CSmH, CtY, DFo, MH, NjP, TxU.

422 - - [Anr.edn]. T. Warren for H. Herringman, sold by R. Bentley, J. Tonson, F. Saunders, and T. Bennet, 1694. 4°. (M 69h)
CLUC, CtY, DFo, ICU, MH, TxU.

DRYDEN, JOHN (continued)

423 - - [Anr.edn.] 1696. 4°. (M 69i) CLUC, CtY, DFo, IEN, TxU.
Second line of imprint ends with "be."

424 - - [Anr.edn.] 1696. 4°. (M.[Osborn]69j) CLUC, DFo.
Imprint reads: "H.Herringman."

425 - - [Anr.edn.] 1696. 4°. (M 69k) CLUC, MH, NIC, TxU.
Imprint reads: "Henry Herringman."

- The Indian queen. 1665; 1692. See Howard, Sir R. *Four new plays,* 1665; *Five new plays,* 1692.

426 - The kind keeper; or, Mr. Limberham. R. Bentley and M. Magnes, 1680. 4°. (M 85a; P 329) CLUC, CSmH, CtY, DFo, DLC, ICN, ICU, MH, MWiW-C, MiU, NjP, NN, **TxU.**

427 - - [Anr.edn.] 1690. 4°. (M 85b) CLUC, CSmH, CtY, DFo, ICN, ICU, IEN, MH, MiU, NIC, NjP, TxU.

428 - King Arthur; or, The British worthy. J. Tonson, 1691. 4°. (M 91ai) CLUC, CSmH, DFo, MH.
No prologue or epilogue.

429 - - [Anr.issue.] 1691. 4°. (M 91aii) CLUC, CSmH, CtY, DFo, DLC, ICN, MH, MWiW-C (variant), NjP, TxU.
With prologue and epilogue. For variants, see Osborn, **p. 92.**

430 - - [Anr.edn.] 1695. 4°. (M 91b) CLUC, CSmH, CtY, DFo, ICN, ICU, MH, MiU, NIC, NjP, TxU.

431 - Love triumphant; or, Nature will prevail. J. Tonson, 1694. 4°. (M 93a) CLUC, CSmH, CtY, DFo, DLC, ICN, ICU, MH, MWiW-C, MiU, NjP, TxU.

- The mall. See *The mall.*

DRYDEN, JOHN (continued)

432 Marriage a-la-mode. T.N. for H. Herringman, 1673. 4°.
     (M 77a; P 330) CLUC, CSmH, CtY, DFo, DLC, ICN, ICU,
     MH, MWiW-C, MiU, NjP, TxU.

433 - - [Anr.edn.] T. N. for H. Herringman, sold by J. Knight and
     F. Saunders, 1684. 4°. (M 77b) CLUC, CSmH, CtY,
     DFo, ICN, ICU, MH, MiU, NjP, TxU.

434 - - [Anr.edn.] E. Jones for H. Herringman, sold by R. Bent-
     ley, 1691. 4°. (M 77c) CLUC, CSmH, CtY, DFo, ICN,
     IEN, MH, MiU, TxU.

435 - - [Anr.edn.] E. Jones for H. Herringman, sold by J. Ton-
     son, F. Saunders, and T. Bennet, 1698. 4°. (M 77d) CLUC,
     CSmH, CtY, DFo, DLC, ICU, MH, TxU.

   - The mistaken husband. See *The mistaken husband*.

436 - Oedipus. R. Bentley and M. Magnes, 1679. 4°. (M 83a;
     P 334) CLUC, CSmH, CtY, DFo, DLC, ICN, ICU, MH,
     MWiW-C, MiU, NjP, NN, TxU.
     In collaboration with N. Lee.

437 - - [Anr.edn.] R. Bentley, 1682. 4°. (M 83b) CLUC, CSmH,
     CtY, DFo, ICU, MH, TxU.

438 - - [Anr.edn.] 1687. 4°. (M 83c) CLUC, CSmH, CtY,
     DFo, ICU, MH, MiU, TxU.

439 - - [Anr.edn.] 1692. 4°. (M 83d) CLUC, CSmH, CtY,
     DFo, ICU, MH, MiU, TxU.

440 - - [Anr.edn.] T. Chapman, [1696.] (M 83e) CLUC, CSmH,
     CtY, DFo, MH, NjP, TxU.

441 - The rival ladies. W.W. for H. Heringman, 1664. 4°. (M67a)
     (M 67a) CLUC, CSmH, CtY, DFo, DLC, MH, MWiW-C,
     NjP, TxU.

442 - - [Anr.edn.] 1669. 4°. (M 67b) CLUC, CSmH, DFo, DLC, ICN, ICU, MH, MiU, TxU.

443 - - [Anr.edn.] T. N. for H. Herringman, 1675. 4°. (M 67c) CLUC, CSmH, CtY, DFo, DLC, ICU, IEN, MH, MiU, NjP, TxU.

444 - - [Anr.edn.] T. W. for H. Herringman, sold by R. Bentley, J. Tonson, F. Saunders, and T. Bennet, 1693. 4°. (M 67d) CLUC, CSmH, CtY, DFo, MH, MiU, TxU.

445 - Secret-love; or, The maiden-queen. H.Herringman, 1668. 4°. (M 70a) CLUC, CSmH, CtY, DFo, MH, MiU, NN, TxU.

446 - - [Anr.edn.] 1669. 4°. (M 70b) CLUC, CSmH, CtY, DFo, ICU, MH, MiU, TxU.
On A2^r, second line from bottom, "giveing"; on B1^r, third line from bottom, "answere."

447 - - [Anr.edn.] 1669. 4°. (Not in M) CSmH, DFo, TxU.
Printed from a different setting of type. On A2^r, second line from bottom, "giving"; on B1^r, third line from bottom, "answer."

448 - - [Anr.edn.] J. M. for H. Herringman, 1675. 4°. (Not in M) CtY.

449 - - [Anr.edn.] 1679. 4°. (M 70c) CLUC, CSmH, CtY, DFo, DLC, ICN, ICU, MH, MiU, NjP, TxU.

450 - - [Anr.edn.] H. Herringman, sold by R. Bentley, 1691. 4°. (M 70d) CLUC, CSmH, CtY, DFo, ICN, ICU, MH, MiU, NN, NjP, PU.

451 - - [Anr.edn.] T. Warren for H. Herringman, sold by J. Tonson, F. Saunders, and T. Bennet, 1698. 4°. (M 70e) CLUC, CtY, DFo, ICU, MH, NIC, TxU.

452 - - [Anr.issue.] T. Warren for H. Herringman, sold by J. Tonson, F. Saunders, T. Bennet, and K. Bentley, 1698. 4°. (Not in M) NIC.

- The secular masque. 1700. See Vanbrugh, J. *The pilgrim.*

453 - Sir Martin Mar-all; or, The feign'd innocence. H. Herringman, 1668. 4°. DFo.
The first issue with uncancelled leaf C2. See M 71a, note.

454 - - [Anr.issue.] 1668. 4°. (M 71a) CLUC, CSmH, CtY, DFo, MH, TxU.

455 - - [Anr.edn.] 1668. 4°. (M 71b) CLUC, CSmH, CtY, DFo, ICN, ICU, MH, MWiW-C, NjP, TxU.

456 - - [Anr.issue.] 1669. 4°. (M 71b) CLUC, CSmH, MH, TxU.
This variant differs from 455 only in the date.

457 - - [Anr.edn.] 1678. 4°. (M 71c) CLUC, CSmH, CtY, DFo, DLC, ICN, ICU, MH, MiU, TxU.

458 - - [Anr.edn.] H. Herringman, sold by F. Saunders, 1691. 4°. (M 71d) CLUC, CSmH, CtY, DFo, ICN, IEN, MH, MiU, NjP.

459 - - [Anr.edn.] T. Warren for H. Herringman, sold by R. Bentley, J. Tonson, F. Saunders, and T. Bennet, 1697. 4°. (M 71e) CLUC, CSmH, CtY, DFo, MH, NIC, PU, TxU.

460 - The Spanish fryar; or, The double discovery. R. Tonson and J. Tonson, 1681. 4°. (Not in M) CSmH, DFo, TxU.
With subtitle set in Roman type.

461 - - [Anr.issue or variant.] 1681. 4°. (M 86a; P 338) CLUC, CSmH, CtY, DFo, DLC, ICN, ICU, MH, MWiW-C, MiU, NjP, TxU.
With subtitle set in Gothic type.

DRYDEN, JOHN (continued)

462 - - [Anr.edn.] 1686. 4°. (M 86b) CLUC, CSmH, CtY,
DFo, ICN, ICU, MH, MiU, TxU.

463 - - [Anr.edn.] 1690. 4°. (M 86c) CLUC, CSmH, CtY,
DFo, ICN, ICU, MH, MiU, NIC, TxU.

464 - - [Anr.edn.] E. Tonson and J. Tonson, 1695. 4°. (M 86d)
CLUC, CSmH, CtY, DFo, IEN, MH, NjP, TxU.

465 - The state of innocence, and fall of man. T.N. for H. Herringman, 1677. 4°. (M 81a) CLUC, CSmH, CtY, DFo, ICU,
MH, NjP, TxU.

466 - - [Anr.edn.] H. H. for H. Herringman, 1678. 4°. (M 81b)
CLUC, CSmH, CtY, DFo, ICN, ICU, MH, NjP, TxU.

467 - - [Anr.edn.] H. H. for H. Herringman, sold by J. Knight and
F. Saunders, 1684. 4°. (M 81c) CSmH, CtY, DFo, DLC,
MH.
Signed A-E⁴, F², G⁴.

468 - - [Anr.edn.] 1684. 4°. (M 81d) CLUC, DFo.
Signed A-E⁴, F², G⁴ (G1 mis-signed F).

469 - - [Anr.edn.] 1684. 4°. (M 81e) CLUC, CSmH, DFo,
DLC, MH.
Signed A-G⁴.

470 - - [Anr.edn.] J. M. for H. Herringman, sold by A. Roper,
1690. 4°. (M 81f) CLUC, CSmH, CtY, DFo, ICU, MH,
TxU.

471 - - [Anr.edn.] H. Herringman, sold by A. Roper, 1692. 4°.
(M 81g) CLUC, CSmH, CtY, DFo, MH, TxU.

472 - - [Anr.edn.] H. Herringman, sold by J. Tonson, F. Saunders,
and T. Bennet, 1695. 4°. (M 81h) CLUC, DFo, TxU.
P. 9, 1.11, misprint "Nigth" for "Night."

DRYDEN, JOHN (continued)

473 - - [Anr.edn.] 1695. 4°. (M 81i) CLUC, CSmH, CtY, DFo, ICU, MH, MiU, NIC, NjP.
P. 9, 1.11, "Night" correctly spelled.

- The tempest. See Davenant, W.

474 - Troilus and Cressida; or, Truth found too late. J. Tonson and A. Swall, 1679. 4°. (M 84ai) CLUC, CSmH, CtY, DFo, DLC, ICN, ICU, MH, MWiW-C, MiU, NIC, NN, PU, TxU.

475 - - [Anr.issue.] A. Swall and J. Tonson, 1679. 4°. (M 81aii; P 915) CLUC, CSmH, DFo, MH, TxU.

476 - - [Anr.edn.] J. Tonson, 1679 [1692?] 4°. (M 84b) CLUC, DFo, MH, TxU.

477 - - [Anr.edn.] I. Dawks for J. Tonson, 1695. 4°. (M 84c) CLUC, CSmH, CtY, DFo, ICN, ICU, MH, MiU, NIC, NjP, PU, TxU.

478 - Tyrannick love; or, The royal martyr. H. Herringman, 1670. 4°. (M 74a) CLUC, CSmH, CtY, DFo, ICU, MH, MiU, MWiW-C, TxU.

479 - - [Anr.issue.] 1670. 4°. (Not in M) CSmH.
Cancelled F3 is replaced by two leaves containing an added scene.

480 - - [Anr.edn.] 1672. 4°. (M 74b) CLUC, CSmH, CtY, DFo, DLC, ICU, MH, NjP, TxU.

481 - - [Anr.edn.] 1677. 4°. (M 74c) CLUC, CtY, DFo, DLC, ICN, ICU, MH, TxU.

482 - - [Anr.edn.] H. Herringman, sold by J. Knight and F. Saunders, 1686. 4°. (M 74d) CLUC, CSmH, CtY, DFo, ICN, ICU, MH, MiU, NIC, NjP, TxU.

DRYDEN, JOHN (continued)

483 - - [Anr.edn.] 1694. 4°. (Not in M) MH.

484 - - [Anr.issue] H. Herringman, sold by R. Bentley, J. Tonson,
F. Saunders, and T. Bennet, 1695. 4°. (M 74e) CLUC,
CSmH, CtY, DFo, DLC, ICN, MH, NIC, TxU.
The title page of this issue is set from the same type as that
of the 1694 issue through "London" in the imprint.

485 - The wild gallant. T. Newcomb for H. Herringman, 1669. 4°.
(M 72a) CLUC, CSmH, CtY, DFo, ICN, MH, NjP, TxU.
"Theatre" on t.-p.

486 - - [Anr.edn.] 1669. 4°. (M 72b; P 340) CLUC, CSmH,
CtY, DFo, DLC, ICU, MH, MWiW-C, TxU.
"Theater" on t.-p.

487 - - [Anr.edn.] H. Hills for H. Herringman, 1684. 4°. (M 72c)
CLUC, CSmH, CtY, DFo, ICN, ICU, MH, MiU, NjP, PU,
TxU.

488 - - [Anr.edn.] 1686. (Summers)

489 - - [Anr.edn.] T. Warren for H. Herringman, sold by R. Bentley, J. Tonson, F. Saunders, and T. Bennet, 1694. 4°. (M 72d)
CLUC, CSmH, CtY, DFo, ICU, MH, MiU, NIC, TxU.

490 DRYDEN, JOHN, junior
The husband his own cuckold. J. Tonson, 1696. 4°. CLUC,
CSmH, CtY, DFo, DLC, ICN, ICU, MH, MWiW-C, MiU,
NN, NjP, TxU.

491 DUFFETT, THOMAS
The amorous old-woman; or, 'Tis well if it take. S. Neale,
1674. 4°. CLUC, CSmH, CtY, ICN.

492 - - [Anr.issue.] S. Neale and B. Tooth, 1674. 4°. DFo, DLC.

493 - - [Anr.issue with cancel title.] The fond lady. S. Neale,
1684. CSmH, DFo, NjP.

54

494   Beauties triumph. 1676. 4°. CSmH, DFo, ICU.

495 - The empress of Morocco. S.Neale,1674. 4°. CLUC, CSmH, CtY, DFo, DLC, ICN, ICU, MH, TxU.

496 - The mock-tempest; or, The enchanted castle. W. Cademan, 1675. 4°. CLUC, CSmH, CtY, DFo, DLC, ICN, MH, MWiW-C, TxU.

497 - Psyche debauch'd. J. Smith, 1678. 4°. CSmH, DFo.

498 - The Spanish rogue. W. Cademan, 1674. 4°. CLUC, CSmH, CtY, DFo, DLC, ICN, ICU, MH, MiU, NjP, TxU.

499 DUNTON, JOHN
    The visions of the soul. J. Dunton, 1692. 8°. CSmH, CtY, ICN, MH.

500 DURFEY, THOMAS
    The banditti; or, A ladies distress. J. B. for R. Bentley and J. Hindmarsh, 1686. 4°. CLUC, CSmH (2 variant copies), CtY, DFo, DLC, ICN, ICU. MH, MiU, NjP.

501 - Bussy D'Ambois; or, The husbands revenge. R. Bently, J. Hindmarsh, and A. Roper, 1691. 4°. CtY, DFo, DLC, ICN, ICU, MH, MiU, TxU.

502 - The campaigners; or, The pleasant adventures at Brussels. A. Baldwin, 1698. 4°. CSmH, CtY, DFo, DLC, ICN, ICU, MH, MWiW-C, MiU, TxU.

503 - The comical history of Don Quixote. 2 parts. S. Briscoe, 1694. 4°. CLUC, CSmH, CtY, DFo, DLC, ICN, ICU, MH, NIC, NN, NjP.
    CBEL and Summers list two edns. or issues of Part I.

504   The comical history of Don Quixote, the third part, with the marriage of Mary the buxome. S. Briscoe, 1696. 4°. CLUC, CSmH, CtY, DFo, DLC, ICN, ICU, MH, NIC, NN, NjP.

DURFEY, THOMAS (continued)

505   A common-wealth of women. R. Bentley and J. Hindmarsh, 1686. 4°. CSmH, CtY, DFo, DLC, ICN, ICU, MH, MiU, NIC, NjP, TxU.

506 - - [Anr.edn.] 1688. 4°. (CBEL, II, 420)

507 - The famous history of the rise and fall of Massaniello. 2 parts. [Part II : The famous history and fall of Massainello; or, A fisherman a prince. 1699.] J. Nutt, 1700, 1699. 4°. CLUC, CSmH, CtY, DFo, ICN, ICU, MH, MiU.

508 - A fond husband; or, The plotting sisters. T. N. for J. Magnes and R. Bentley, 1677. 4°. CSmH, CtY, DFo, DLC, ICN, ICU, MH, NjP.

509 - - [Anr.edn.] R. E. for J. Magnes and R. Bentley, 1678. 4°. CSmH, DFo, DLC, ICN, MH, MiU, TxU.

510 - - [Anr.edn.] R. E. for R. Bentley and S. Magnes, 1685. 4°. CtY, DFo, ICU, MH, NN, NjP.

511 - The fool turn'd critick. J. Magnes and R. Bentley, 1678. 4°. (P 343) CLUC, CSmH, CtY, DFo, DLC, ICN, ICU, MH, MWiW-C, MiU, NjP, TxU.

512 - A fool's preferment; or, The three Dukes of Dunstable. J. Knight and F. Saunders, 1688. 4°. (P 344) CLUC, CSmH, CtY, DFo, DLC, ICN, ICU, MH, MWiW-C, MiU, TxU.

513 - The injured princess; or, The fatal wager. R. Bentley and M. Magnes, 1682. 4°. CSmH, CtY, DFo, DLC, ICN, ICU, MH, MiU, NjP, PU, TxU.

514 - The intrigues at Versailles; or, A jilt in all humours. F. Saunders, P. Buck, R. Parker, and H. Newman, 1697. 4°. CLUC, CSmH, CtY, DFo, DLC, ICN, ICU, MH, NjP, TxU.

515 - - [Anr.edn.] 1697. (CBEL, II, 421)

516   Love for money; or, The boarding school. A. Roper, sold by
R. Taylor, 1691. 4°. (P 346) CLUC, CSmH, CtY, DFo,
*DLC, ICN, ICU, MH, MiU, NjP, *PU.
> Signed A⁴, π¹, B-H⁴, K¹. One variant of the title-page
> bears the words, "As it is acted at the Theatre Royal;" the
> other variant replaces these words with a triangular orna-
> **ment.**

517 - - [Anr.edn.] 1691. 4°.
> Signed A-H⁴. See P 346, note.

518 - - [Anr.edn.] J. Hindmarsh, A. Roper, sold by R. Taylor, 1691.
4°. **CSmH.**

519 - - [Anr.edn.] A. Roper, E. Wilkinson, and J. Hindmarsh, 1696.
4°. CtY, DFo, DLC, ICU, MH, MWiW-C, TxU.

520 - Madam Fickle; or, The witty false one. T. N. for J. Magnes
and R. Bentley, 1677. 4°. (P 347) CLUC, CSmH, CtY,
ICN, ICU, MH, MWiW-C, MiU.

521 - - [Anr.edn.] R. Bentley, 1682. 4°. CtY, DFo, DLC, ICN,
ICU, MH, PU.

522 - - [Anr.edn.] R. Bentley, 1691. 4°. CtY, DFo, ICN, MH.

523 - The marriage-hater match'd. R. Bentley, 1692. 4°. CSmH,
DFo, DLC, ICU, MH, MiU.

524 - - [Anr.issue.] R. Parker and S. Briscoe, 1692. 4°. CtY, NjP.

525 - - [Anr.edn.] R. Bentley, R. Parker, and S. Briscoe, 1693. 4°.
CLUC, CtY, DFo, DLC, ICN, ICU, MH, MiU, NN, TxU.

526 - A new opera call'd Cinthia and Endimion. W. Onley for S.
Briscoe and R. Wellington, 1697. 4°. CLUC, CSmH, DFo,
DLC, ICU, MH, MiU, NjP.

DURFEY, THOMAS (continued)

527 - - [Anr.edn.] 1697. 4°. CSmH, ICN.
"The second edition;" running-title on D2r, "nnd."

528 - The Richmond heiress; or, A woman once in the right. S.
Briscoe, 1693. 4°. CSmH, DFo.
Issue with "Theatre Roayl . . . by Tho. D'Urfey, Gent."
on title; signed A-I⁴; erratic pagination, 1-32, 29-36, 41-64;
and early state of text. See Huth sale catalogue.

529 - - [Anr.issue.] 1693. 4°. CLUC, CSmH, CtY, DLC, ICN,
ICU, MH, MWiW-C, MiU, NjP, TxU.
"Theatre Royal . . . by Mr. D'Urfey" on title; corrected
pagination; altered and amended text. The Huth copy is
described as having five leaves in the A gathering; the
Thorn-Drury copy wanted the "inserted leaf I3."

530 - The royalist. J. Hindmarsh, 1682. 4°. (P 348) CLUC,
CSmH, CtY, DFo, DLC, ICN, ICU, MH, MWiW-C, MiU,
NjP, TxU.

531 - The siege of Memphis; or, The ambitious queen. W. Cademan, 1676. 4°. CLUC, CSmH, CtY, DFo, DLC, ICN,
ICU, MH, MWiW-C, MiU, NjP, TxU.

532 - Sir Barnaby Whigg; or, No wit like a womans. A. G. and
J. P. for J. Hindmarsh, 1681. 4°. CLUC, CSmH, CtY, DFo,
DLC, ICN, ICU, MH, MWiW-C, MiU, NjP, TxU.

533 - Squire Oldsapp; or, The night-adventurers. J. Magnes and R.
Bentley, 1679. 4°. (P 349) CLUC, CSmH, CtY, DFo,
DLC, ICN, ICU, MH, MWiW-C, MiU, NjP, TxU.

534 - Trick for trick; or, The debauch'd hypocrite. L. Curtiss, 1678.
4°. CSmH, CtY, DFo, DLC, ICN, ICU, NjP.

535 - The virtuous wife; or, Good luck at last. T. N. for R. Bentley and M. Magnes, 1680. 4°. CLUC, CSmH, CtY, DFo,
DLC, ICN, ICU, MH, MWiW-C, MiU, NN, NjP, TxU.

536 ECCLESTONE, EDWARD
>Noah's flood; or, The destruction of the world. M. Clark and sold by B. Tooke, 1679. 4°. CSmH, CtY, DFo, DLC, ICN, **ICU, MH.**

537 - - [Anr.issue with changed title.] The cataclysm; or, General deluge of the world. T. M. and sold by I. Holford, 1685. 4°. **CSmH, DLC, MWiW-C.**

538 - - [Anr.issue with changed title.] The deluge. 1690. 4°. **British Museum.**

539 ECHARD, LAWRENCE
>Plautus's comedies: Amphitryon, Epidicus and Rudens made English. A. Swalle and T. Child, 1694. 8°. CLUC, CSmH, CtY, DFo, DLC (Rudens only), ICN, ICU, IEN, MH, MiU, NN, NjP, TxU.

540 - Terence's comedies made English. A. Swall and T. Childe, 1694. 8°. CSmH, CtY, DFo, ICN, MH, MiU.

541 - - [Anr.edn.] T. Child, 1698. 12°. British Museum.

>EDMONTON. See *The merry devil of Edmonton.*

542 EMILIA. For the author, 1672. 8°. CSmH.

543 ETHEREGE, SIR GEORGE
>The comical revenge; or, Love in a tub. H. Herringman, 1664. 4°. CSmH, DFo, MWiW-C, TxU.
>**Pp. viii,92,ii.**

544 - - [Anr.edn.] 1664. 4°. CLUC, CtY, MH, TxU.
>**Pp. vi,71,iii.**

545 - - [Anr.edn.] H. Herringman, 1667. 4°. CSmH, DFo, ICN, **ICU, TxU.**

546 - - [Anr.edn.]   H. Herringman, 1669. 4°. CSmH, DFo, ICU.
 In title: "Revenge;... Lincolns-Inn-Fields."

547 - - [Anr.edn.]   1669. 4°. CSmH, CtY, DFo, ICN, MH, NIC,
 NN, PU, TxU.
 In title: "Revenge,... Lincolns-Inn-fields."

548 - - [Anr.edn.]   H. Herringman, sold by F. Saunders, 1689. 4°.
 CLUC, CtY, DFo, ICU, MH, MiU.

549 - - [Anr.issue with cancel title-page.]   H. Herringman, sold by
 S. Manship, 1690. 4°. CLUC, CSmH, DFo, MH.

550 - - [Anr.edn.]   T. Warren for H. Herringman, sold by J. Tonson, G. Saunders, T. Bennet, and K. Bentley, 1697. 4°. CtY,
 DFo, ICN, MH, MiU.

551 - The man of mode; or, Sʳ Fopling Flutter. J. Macock for H.
 Herringman, 1676. 4°. (P 360) CLUC, CSmH, CtY, DFo,
 DLC, ICN, ICU, MH, MWiW-C, MiU, NjP, TxU.

552 - - [Anr.edn.]   J. Macock for H. Herringman, sold by J. Knight
 and F. Saunders, 1684. 4°. CLUC, CtY, MH, *TxU.
 Head-title on [A4] in italic.

553 - - [Anr.issue.]   DFo, ICU, MH, MiU.
 Head-title on [A4] in Roman.

554 - - [Anr.edn.]   T. Warren for H. Herringman, sold by R. Bentley, J. Tonson, F. Saunders, and T. Bennet, 1693. 4°. CLUC,
 DFo, MH.

555 - She wou'd if she cou'd. H. Herringman, 1668. 4°. (P 361)
 CSmH, CtY, DFo, ICN, ICU, MH, MWiW-C, NjP, TxU.

556 - - [Anr.edn.]   T. N. for H. Herringman, 1671. 4°. CtY, DFo,
 DLC, MH, MiU, TxU.

ETHEREGE, SIR GEORGE (continued)
557 - - [Anr.edn.]   T. Warren for H. Herringman, sold by R. Bentley, J. Tonson, F. Saunders, and T. Bennet, 1693. 4°. CSmH, CtY, DFo, MH, TxU.

AN EXCELLENT COMEDY, CALLD, THE PRINCE OF PRIGGS REVELS. See S., J.

557a THE EXTRAVAGANT SHEEPHERD. [Tr.T.R.] J.G. for T.Heath,1654. 4°. CLUC, CSmH, DFo, ICN.

THE FACTIOUS CITIZEN. See *Mr. Turbulent.*

THE FAIRY QUEEN. See Settle, E.

558 THE FAMOUS TRAGEDIE OF KING CHARLES I. Printed in the year, 1649. 4°. DFo, DLC, ICN, MH.

559 FANE, SIR FRANCIS
Love in the dark ; or, The man of bus'ness. T. N. for H. Herringman, 1675. 4°. CLUC, CSmH, CtY, DFo, DLC, ICN, ICU, MH, MWiW-C, MiU, NjP, TxU.

560 - - [Anr.issue.]   1671, [i.e. 1675.] 4°. CSmH.

561 - Mask. In *Poems* by N. Tate. J. Hindmarsh, 1685. 8°. DFo.

562 - The sacrifice. J. R. for J. Weld, 1686. 4°. CSmH, CtY, DFo, DLC, ICU.

563 - - [Anr.edn.]   1687. 4°. DLC, MH, MiU, NjP, TxU.

564 - - [Anr.edn.]   1687. 4°. DFo, ICN, MH.
        "Third edition."

FANSHAWE, SIR RICHARD
Fida pastora. See Beaumont, F. and J. Fletcher. *The faithfull shepherdesse.* 1658.

- Fiestas di Aranjuez. In his *Querer por solo querer.* 1670; 1671.

FANSHAWE, SIR RICHARD (continued)
Il pastor fido.   See Guarini, G. B.

565 - Querer por solo querer: To love only for love sake.   W. Godbid, 1670.   4°.   (P 362A)   CSmH, DFo, DLC.
Paraphrased from the Spanish of Don Antonio de Mendoza.

566 - - [Anr.issue with cancel title.]   W. Godbid, sold by M. Pitt,
1671.   4°.   CSmH, DFo, ICN, MH.

567 FARQUHAR, GEORGE
The constant couple; or, A trip to the jubilee.   R. Smith and
B. Banbury, 1700.   4°.   MH, MWiW-C.

568 - - [Anr.edn.]   R.Smith, C. and B.Banbury,1700.   4°.   DFo.
The second edn., with added scene.

569 - Love and a bottle.   R. Standfast and F. Coggen, 1699.   4°.
CSmH, DFo, DLC, ICN, MH, MWiW-C, TxU.

570 THE FATAL DISCOVERY; or, Love in ruines.   J.Orme for
R. Wellington, sold by P. Gilborne and B. Lintott, 1698.   4°.
CSmH, DFo, ICN, MH, TxU.
Epilogue, 12 1. on p. 50.

571 - - [Anr.issue.]   CLUC, CSmH.
No epilogue.

572 THE FEIGN'D ASTROLOGER.   T. Thornycroft, 1668.   4°.
CSmH, CtY, DLC, ICN, MiU.
Translated from T. Corneille.

573 FEIGN'D FRIENDSHIP; or, The mad reformer.   D. Brown,
F.Coggan, E.Rumballd, and R.Gibson, [1698 or 1699?]   4°.
CSmH, CtY, DFo, DLC, ICU, MiU, NjP.

574 THE FEMALE WITS; or, The triumvirate of poets at rehearsal.   1697.   4°.   CSmH.

FILMER, EDWARD
Pompey the great.   1664.   See Waller, E.

FILMER, EDWARD (continued)
575   The unnatural brother. J. Orme for R. Wilkin, 1697. 4°.
    CSmH, CtY, DFo, DLC, ICN, ICU, MH, MiU, NjP, TxU.

576 FLECKNOE, RICHARD
    Ariadne deserted by Theseus. Printed anno Dom. 1654. 8°.
    CSmH.

577 - The damoiselles a la mode. For the author, 1667. 8°. CSmH,
    DFo.

578 - Erminia ; or, The fair and virtuous lady. For the author, 1661.
    8°. CSmH.

579 - - [Anr.edn.] W. Crook, 1665. 8°. DFo.

580 - Love's dominion. Printed in the year 1654. 8°. CLUC,
    CSmH, MH, TxU.

581 - [Anr.edn. with changed title.] Love's kingdom. R. Wood
    for the author, 1664. 8°. CSmH, CtY, DFo, DLC, MH,
    MiU.

582 - - [Anr.issue with cancel title-page.] S. Neale, 1674. 8° CSmH,
    DFo.

583 -The marriage of Oceanus and Britannia. Printed anno 1659.
    12°. CSmH.

584 FLEMING, ROBERT
    Monarchical image. J. A. for J. Salusbury, 1691. 8°. In his
    Mirrour of divine love. CSmH, CtY, DFo, DLC.

    FLETCHER, JOHN. See also Beaumont, F. and J. Fletcher.
    Bonduca. See Powell, G.

585 - The island princess; or, The generous Portugal. H. R. and
    A. M., sold by W. Cademan and R. Pask, 1669. 4°. CLUC,
    CSmH, CtY, DFo, DLC, ICN, MH, MiU.

FLETCHER, JOHN (continued)
- - [Anr.edn.] 1687. See Tate, N.

- - [Anr.edn.] 1699. See Motteux, P. A.

FORD, JOHN
>The witch of Edmonton. See Rowley, W., T. Dekker and
>J. Ford.

586 FORD, JOHN and THOMAS DEKKER
>The sun's-darling. J. Bell for A. Penneycuicke, 1656. 4°.
>(P 281) CSmH, CtY, DLC, MH.
>>At least four different dedications are found singly in copies
>>of this issue: la, to the Earl of Southampton—the Morgan
>>Library; 1b, to the Earl of Southampton, from a different
>>setting of type — the Pforzheimer Library; 2, to the Earl
>>of Kingston — Bodley; 3, to Lady Newton — Dyce Col-
>>lection; and 4, to the Earl of Northumberland — Wise
>>copy at the British Museum.

587 - - [Anr.issue.] J. Bell for A. Penneycuicke, 1657. 4°. (P 281,
>notes) CSmH, CtY.

588 - - [Anr.issue.] CSmH, DFo, DLC, MH.
>This issue omits reference to performances at Whitehall
>on the title-page.

589 FORDE, THOMAS
>Love's labyrinth; or, The royal shepherdess. R. and W. Ley-
>bourn for W. Grantham, 1660. 8°. In his *Virtus rediviva*,
>1661. CSmH, DFo, DLC, ICN, ICU, MH, MWiW-C, NjP
>(bound separately).

590 FOUNTAIN, JOHN
>The rewards of vertue. J. Cottrel for H. Fletcher, 1661. 4°.
>CSmH, ICU, MH, MiU.

591 FOXE, JOHN
>Christus triumphans. Impensis R. Clavel, 1672. 8°. CSmH,
>DFo.

FOXE, JOHN (continued)

592 Entry cancelled.

593 - - [Anr.edn.] 1677. 8°. (DNB)

594 FREEMAN, SIR RALPH
Imperiale. T. Harper, sold by R. Pollard, 1655. 4°. CLUC,
CSmH, CtY, DFo, DLC, ICN, ICU, MH, MiU, NIC, PU,
TxU.

GAMMER GURTON'S NEEDLE. See S., Mr., Mr. of Art.

595 GAYTON, EDMUND
Charity triumphant; or, The virgin show. N. Brooke, 1655.
4°. British Museum.

596 GESTA GRAYORUM ... together with a masque. W. Canning, 1688. 4°. DFo.

597 THE GHOST; or, The woman wears the breeches. W. Bentley for T. Heath, 1653. 4°. CSmH, CtY, DLC, ICN, ICU,
MWiW-C, TxU.

598 GILDON, CHARLES
Measure for measure; or, Beauty the best advocate. D. Brown
and R. Parker, 1700. 4°. CSmH, CtY, DFo, MH, MiU,
PU.

599 - Phaeton; or, The fatal divorce. A. Roper, 1698. 4°. CSmH,
CtY, DFo, DLC, ICN, ICU, MH, MiU, NjP.

600 - The Roman brides revenge. J. Sturton, 1697. 4°. CSmH,
CtY, DFo, DLC, ICN, MH.

GODOLPHIN, SIDNEY
Pompey the great. 1664. See Waller, E.

601 GOFFE, THOMAS
Three excellent tragoedies. Viz. The raging Turk; or, Bajazet
the second. The courageous Turk; or, Amurath the first.

And the tragoedie of Orestes. G. Bedell and T. Collins, 1656. 8°. CSmH, CtY, DFo, DLC, ICN, ICU, MH, NIC, PU, **TxU.**

602 - The careles shepherdess. R. Rogers and W. Ley, 1656. 4°. *CSmH, *CtY, DFo, DLC, ICN, ICU, *MH, *MWiW-C.

603 - - [Anr.issue.] The careless shepherdes. 1656. 4°. DFo, **DLC.**

- The courageous Turk. In his *Three excellent tragoedies.*

- The raging Turk. In his *Three excellent tragoedies.*

- The tragoedie of Orestes. In his *Three excellent tragoedies.*

GOLDSMITH, FRANCIS. See Grotius, H.

604 THE GOSSIPS BRAULE; or, The women wear the breeches. Printed 1655. British Museum.

605 GOULD, ROBERT
The rival sisters; or, The violence of love. R. Bently, F. Saunders, and J. Knapton, 1696. 4°. CLUC, CSmH, CtY, DFo, DLC, ICN, ICU, MH, MiU, NN, NjP, TxU.

606 GRANVILLE, GEORGE, Lord Lansdowne
Heroick love. F.Saunders. H.Playford, and B.Tooke,1698. 4°. CLUC, CSmH, CtY, DFo, DLC, ICN, ICU, MH, MWiW-C, NN, NjP, PU, TxU.

607 - The she-gallants. H. Playford and B. Tooke, 1696. 4°. (P 423) CLUC, CSmH, CtY, DFo, DLC, ICN, ICU, MH, NjP, TxU.

608 GRATIAE THEATRALES; or, A choice ternary of English plays, viz.: Thorny-Abbey; or, The London-maid. Written by T. W.: The marriage-broker; or, The pander. Written by M. W.; Grim the collier of Croyden; or, The devil and his dame; with the devil and Saint Dunstan. By I. T. R. D., 1662. 12°. CLUC, CSmH, DFo, ICN, ICU.

609 GREENE, ALEXANDER
The polititian cheated. R.Crofts, 1663. 4°. (P 424) CSmH, DFo, DLC, ICN, ICU, MH, MWiW-C.

610 GREENE, ROBERT
The honorable history of frier Bacon and frier Bungay. J. Bell, 1655. 4°. (G 121c) CSmH, DFo.

611 GREENE, ROBERT and THOMAS LODGE
Lady alimony; or, The alimony lady. T. Vere and W. Gilbertson, 1659. 4°. (P 575) CSmH, CtY, DFo, DLC, ICN, MH.

GRIM THE COLLIER OF CROYDON. In *Gratiae theatrales*.

612 GROTIUS, HUGO
Christ's passion, tr. G.Sandys. J.R. for T.Basset,1687. 8°. CSmH, CtY, DFo, DLC, ICN, ICU, MH, NIC, NjP, PU. "The 2d edn., illustrated."

613 - - [Anr.edn.] J. Blare, 1698. 8°. British Museum.

614 - His Sophompaneas; or, Joseph, with annotations by F. Goldsmith. W. H. and sold by J. Hardesty, [1652.] 8°. CSmH, CtY, DFo, DLC, ICN, MH, MWiW-C, NIC, NN.

615 GUARINI, GIOVANNI BATTISTA
Il pastor fido, tr. R. Fanshawe. R. Raworth, 1647. 4°. CLUC, CSmH, DLC, MH, NIC, NjP, PU, TxU.

616 - - [Anr.issue.] H.Moseley,1648. 4°. CSmH, CtY, DFo, DLC, ICN, ICU, IEN, MH, MWiW-C, NjP, NN, TxU.

617 - - [Anr.edn.] A. Moseley, 1664. 8°. CSmH, CtY, MH.

618 - - [Anr.edn.] H. Herringman, 1676. 8°. CSmH, DFo, ICU, IEN, MH, MiU, TxU.

618a - - [Anr.issue with cancel title-page.] R.Bentley,1692. DFo.

- - [Anr.edn.] 1677. See Settle, E.

GUY, EARL OF WARWICK. See J., B.

619 HACKET, JOHN
Loiola. Typis R. C., sumptibus A. Crooke, 1648. 12 mo. CtY, DFo, ICN, MH, PU.
> Contains also *Stoicus vapulans, Cancer,* and T. Vincent's *Paria,* each with title-page; but signatures and pagination are continuous.

620 HARRIS, JOSEPH
The city bride; or, The merry cuckold. A. Roper and E. Wilkinson, 1696. 4°. CSmH, DFo, DLC.

621 - Love's a lottery, and a woman the prize, with a new masque call'd Love and riches reconcil'd. D. Brown and E. Rumball, 1699. 4°. CSmH, CtY, DLC, ICN, ICU, MH, MiU.

622 - The mistakes; or, The false report. J. Hindmarsh, 1691. 4°. CLUC, CSmH, CtY, DFo, DLC, ICN, ICU, MH, MiU, NjP.

HAUGHTON, WILLIAM
Lusts dominion. See Marlowe, C.

623 HAYNES, JOSEPH
A fatal mistake; or, The plot spoil'd. T. H., sold by R. Taylor, 1692. 4°. MH.

624 - - [Anr.edn.] S. Briscoe, sold by E. Whitlock, 1696. 4°. CLUC, CSmH, DFo, DLC, ICN, ICU, TxU.

625 HEAD, RICHARD
Hic et ubique; or, The humors of Dublin. R.D.,1663. 4°. CSmH, DFo, DLC.

THE HECTORS. 1656. See Prestwich, E.

HEMING, WILLIAM
The eunuch. See no. 629.

626 - The fatal contract. J. M., 1653. 4°. CSmH, CtY, DFo, DLC, ICN, PU, TxU.

HEMING, WILLIAM (continued)

627 - - [Anr.issue.] A. Pennycuicke, 1654. 4°. CSmH, DFo, MH, TxU.

628 - - [Anr.edn.] R. Gammon, 1661. 4°. CSmH, DFo, ICU, MH, TxU.

629 - - [Anr.edn. with changed title.] The eunuch. J. B., sold by R. Taylor, 1687. 4°. CSmH, CtY, DFo, ICN, ICU, MH, MiU, NIC, TxU.

630 - The Jewes tragedy; or, Their fatal and final overthrow by Vespatian and Titus his son. M.Inman, sold by R.Gammon, 1662. 4°. CSmH (2 variant copies), CtY, DFo, DLC, MH, TxU.

631 HEYWOOD, THOMAS
Fortune by land and sea. J. Sweeting and R. Pollard, 1655. 4°. CSmH, CtY, DFo, DLC, ICN, ICU, MH, PU.

632 - Loves mistress; or, The queens masque. J. Raworth for J. Crouch, 1640 [*rectius* c.1662.] (STC 13354) CSmH, CtY, DFo, MH.
Signed A-G⁴. See R. C. Bald, *MP* 41 (1943). 26.

633 HIGDEN, HENRY
The wary widdow; or, Sir Noisy Parrat. A. Roper and T. Rainy, 1693. 4°. CLUC, CSmH, DFo, DLC, ICN, MH, MiU, TxU.

634 HOLLAND, SAMUEL
Venus and Adonis. 1656. 8°. In his *Wit and fancy in a maze*. T. W. for T. Vere, 1656. CSmH, DFo.

635 - - [Anr.issue.] 1660. 8°. In his *Romancio-Mastrix*. Printed for the author, 1660. CSmH.

636 HOOLE, CHARLES
Comoediae sex Anglo-Latinae ... Six comedies. (Andria, Eunuchus, Heautontimorumenos, Adelphi, Hecyra, Phormio).

Company of Stationers, 1663. 4°. CSmH.
Translated from Terence.

637 - - [Anr.edn.] J. F1. for the Company of Stationers, 1667. 4°.
MH.

638 - - [Anr.edn.] E. F. for the Company of Stationers, 1676. 4°.
ICN, ICU, NIC.

639 HOPKINS, CHARLES
Boadicea queen of Britain. J. Tonson, 1697. 4°. CLUC,
**CSmH, CtY, DFo, DLC, ICN, ICU, MH, MiU, NIC, NjP,
PU, TxU.**

640 - Friendship improv'd; or, The female warriour. J. Tonson,
1700. 4°. CLUC, CSmH, CtY, DFo, DLC, ICN, ICU,
MH, MiU, NjP, PU, TxU.

641 - Neglected virtue; or, The unhappy conquerour. H. Rhodes,
R. Parker, and S. Briscoe, 1696. 4°. CSmH, CtY, DFo,
DLC, ICN, ICU, MH, MWiW-C, MiU, NjP.

642 - Pyrrhus king of Epirus. S. Briscoe, P. Buck, and D. Dring,
1695. 4°. CLUC, CSmH, CtY, DFo, DLC, ICN, ICU, MH,
MWiW-C, MiU, NjP, PU, TxU.

HORDEN, HILDEBRAND.
Neglected virtue. See Hopkins, C.

643 HOWARD, EDWARD
The man of Newmarket. J. C. for W. Crook, 1678.   4°.
CSmH, CtY, DLC, ICN, ICU, MH, MiU.

644 - The six days adventure; or, The new Utopia. T. Dring, 1671.
4°. CSmH, CtY, DFo, DLC, ICN, ICU, MH, MiU, NjP,
TxU.

645 - The usurper. H. Herringman, 1668. 4°. CLUC, CSmH, CtY,
DFo, DLC, ICN, ICU, MH, MWiW-C, MiU, NN, NjP,
TxU.

HOWARD, EDWARD (continued)

646   The womens conquest.   J. M. for H. Herringman, 1671.   4°.
CLUC, CSmH, CtY, DFo, DLC, ICN, ICU, MH, MWiW-C,
MiU, NjP, PU, TxU.

647 HOWARD, JAMES
All mistaken; or, The mad couple. H.Brugis for J.Magnes,
1672. 4°. CLUC, CSmH, CtY, DFo, DLC, ICN, ICU,
MH, MWiW-C, MiU, NjP, TxU.

648 - The English mounsieur. H. Bruges for J. Magnus, 1674. 4°.
CLUC, CSmH, CtY, DFo, DLC, ICN, ICU, MH, MiU,
NjP, TxU.

649 - - [Anr.edn.]   W. Cademan, 1679. 8°.   British Museum.

650 HOWARD, SIR ROBERT
Four new plays: The surprisal, The committee, The Indian-
queen, The vestal-virgin.   H. Herringman, 1665.   fol.
(M 68a) CLUC, CSmH, CtY, DFo, DLC, ICN, ICU, IEN,
MH, MWiW-C, NIC, NjP, PU, TxU.

651 - Five new plays: The surprisal, The committee, The Indian-
queen, The vestal-virgin, The Duke of Lerma. H. Herringman, sold by R. Bentley, J. Tonson, F. Saunders, and T. Bennet, 1692. fol. (M [Osborne] 68biii) CSmH, DFo, DLC.

652 - - [Anr.issue.] H. Herringman, sold by T. Bennet, 1692. fol.
(M 68bi) CLUC, CSmH, CtY, ICN, ICU, MiU.
"The second edition corrected."

653 - - [Anr.issue.]   H. Herringman, sold by F. Saunders, 1692.
fol. (M 68bii)

654 - - [Anr.issue.] H. Herringman, sold by J. Tonson, D. Browne,
T. Bennet, and R. Wellington, 1700. fol. CtY, DFo, ICU,
MH, TxU.

655 - The blind lady. H. Herringman, 1660. 8°. In his *Poems*,
1660. (M 4a ;P 511) CLUC, CSmH, CtY, DFo, DLC, ICN,
ICU, MH.

656 - - [Anr.issue with cancel title.]   F. Saunders, 1696. 8°.   In his *Poems,* 1696.   (M 4b; P 511)   CLUC, DFo, MH.

- The committee.   1665.   See his *Four new plays.*

- - [Anr.edn.]   1692.   See his *Five new plays.*

- The Duke of Lerma.   See his *The great favorite; Five new plays.*

657 - The great favourite; or, The Duke of Lerma. H.Herringman, 1668.   4°.   CLUC, CSmH, CtY, DFo, DLC, ICN, ICU, MH, MWiW-C, TxU.

- The Indian-queen.   1665.   See his *Four new plays.*

- - [Anr.edn.]   1692.   See his *Five new plays.*

- The surprisal.   1665.   See his *Four new plays.*

- - [Anr.edn.]   1692.   See his *Five new plays.*

- The vestal-virgin; or, The Roman ladies.   1665.   See his *Four new plays.*

- - [Anr.edn.]   1692.   See his *Five new plays.*

658 HOWELL, JAMES
The nuptialls of Peleus and Thetis. 2 parts. H.Herringman, 1654.   4°.   CLUC, CSmH, CtY, DFo, DLC, ICN, MH, MiU, PU.

659 THE HUNTINGDON DIVERTISEMENT; or, An enterlude for the generall entertainment of the county-feast, held at Merchant-taylors Hall, June 20, 1678.   J. Bennet, 1678.   4°. CSmH (2 variant copies), ICU.

HURLADO DE MENDOZA, ANTONIO.   See Fanshawe, R.

THE IMPERIAL TRAGEDY.   See Killigrew, W.

660 IRENA. R. White for O. Pulleyn, Jr., 1664. 4°. CSmH.

THE ISLAND PRINCESS. 1669. See Fletcher, J.

THE ISLAND PRINCESS. 1687. See Tate, N.

THE ISLAND PRINCESS. 1699. See Motteux, P.

661 J., B.
    The tragical history, admirable atchievments, and various events of Guy Earl of Warwick. T. Vere and W. Gilbertson, 1661. 4°. DFo.

JAQUES, FRANCIS. See Aristophanes.

662 JEVON, THOMAS
    The devil of a wife; or, A comical transformation. J. Heptinstall for J. Eaglesfield, 1686. 4°. CLUC, CSmH, CtY, DFo, DLC, MH, MiU, TxU.

663 - - [Anr.edn.] J. Knapton, 1693. 4°. DFo, ICN, MH, NjP.

664 - - [Anr.edn.] J. Knapton, 1695. CSmH, DFo, ICU, MH, NjP, PU, TxU.
    4 p.1., 47p. CSmH has another copy of this edn. with variant readings.

665 - - [Anr.edn.] J. Knapton, 1695. DLC.
    3 p.1., 42p.

666 JOHNS, WILLIAM
    The traitor to him-self; or, Mans heart his greatest enemy. Oxford, L.L., sold by E. Forrest and H. Keat, 1678. 4°. CSmH, DFo, MH.

667 JONSON, BENJAMIN
    The works. T. Hodgkin, for H. Herringman, E. Brewster, T. Bassett, R. Chiswell, M. Wotton, G. Conyers, 1692. fol. (P 561) CSmH, DFo, DLC, ICN, ICU, MH, MiU, NIC, NjP, TxU.

JONSON, BENJAMIN (continued)

668   Catiline his conspiracy. A. C. sold by W. Cademan, 1669. 4°. (G 296f; P 542) CLUC, CSmH, CtY, DFo, DLC, MH, MWiW-C, NIC, NjP.

669 - - [Anr.edn.] W. Crook, 1674. 4°. (G 296gᵗ) DFo, ICU, **MH.**

670 - - [Anr.issue.] A. C. sold by W. Cademan, 1674. 4°. (G 296g*) CSmH, CtY, ICN, TxU.

671 - The divil is an asse. Imprinted at London, 1641. fol. In his *The workes*. The second volume, 1640. CSmH, CtY, DFo, IEN, TxU.
    See P 560, notes.

672 - - [Anr.issue.] Imprinted London, and are to be sold in Fleet-street, and Westminster-Hall, 1669. fol. In his *The workes*. The second volume, 1640. Welbeck Abbey.

673 - The sad shepherd. Printed 1641. fol. In his *The workes*. The second volume, 1640. CSmH, DFo, ICN, ICU, MH, MWiW-C.

674 JONSON, BENJAMIN, JOHN FLETCHER and THOMAS MIDDLETON
    The widdow. H. Moseley, 1652. 4°. CSmH, DFo, DLC, ICN, ICU, MH, PU, TxU.

675 JORDAN, THOMAS
    Bacchus festival; or, A new medley. 1660. (CBEL I, 646; Nicoll 365).

676 - The cheaters cheated. 1659. 8°. In his *A rosarie of rarities planted in the garden of poetry*. For the author, 1659. Bodley.

677 - - [Anr.issue.] 1663. 8°. In his *A royal arbor of loyal poesie, consisting of poems and songs. Digested into triumph, elegy, satyr, love & drollery*. R. W. for E. Andrews, 1663. DFo.

678 - - [Anr.issue.] [c.1665.] 8°. In his *Nursery of novelties in variety of poetry*. For the author, [c.1665.] British Museum, Bodley.

679 - Cupid his coronation. 1657. 4°. In his *Fancy's festivals,* 1657. DFo.

680 - Ecologue, or representation in four parts, composed for the lord mayor ... 1659. 1659. 8°. In his *A rosarie of rarities,* 1659. Bodley.

681 - - [Anr.issue.] 1663. 8°. In his *A royal arbor of loyal poesie,* 1663. DFo.

682 - - [Anr.issue.] [c.1665.] 8°. In his *Nursery of novelties,* [c.1665.] British Museum, Bodley.

683 - Fancy's festivals. T. Wilson, 1657. 4°. CLUC, DFo.

684 - The goldsmiths jubile; or London's triumphs. W. Godbid for J. Playford, 1674. 4°. (P 563) CSmH.

685 - London in its splendor. W. G. for M. Brooks and J. Playford, 1673. 4°. CtY.

686 - London in luster; projecting many bright beams of triumph. J. Playford, 1679. 4°. CLUC, CSmH, CtY, DLC, ICN, MH.

687 - London triumphant; or, The city in jollity and splendor. W. G. for N. Brook and J. Playford, 1672. 4°. CSmH.
      Without "postscript."

688 - - [Anr.issue.] 1672. CSmH, MH.
      With "postscript."

689 - London's glory. J. and H. Playford, 1680. 4°. CSmH, ICN, MH.

JORDAN, THOMAS (continued)

690   London's joy; or, The Lord Mayors show. J. and H. Playford, 1681. 4°. CSmH, ICN.

691 - London's resurrection to joy and triumph. H. Brome, 1671. 4°. CSmH, MH.
     1 p. 1., 20p.

692 - - [2nd edn.] 1671. CLUC, CSmH.
     1 p. 1., 22p.; imprint MDCLXXI.

693 - London's royal triumph. J. and H. Playford, 1684. 4°. CSmH.

694 - London's triumphs. J. Playford, 1676. 4°. CSmH.

695 - Londons triumphs. J. Playford, 1677. 4°. CSmH, DFo, DLC, ICN.

696 - The lord mayor's show. T. Burnel, 1682. 4°. CSmH.

697 - Money is an asse. P. Lillicrap for F. Kirkman, 1668. 4°. CSmH, DFo, DLC, MH, NN.

698 - A new droll; or, The counter-scuffle. The second part. Printed for the reader's recreation, 1663. 4° DFo.

699 - The triumphs of London. J. Macock for J. Playford, 1675. 4°. CLUC, CSmH, ICN.

700 - The triumphs of London. J. Playford, 1678. 4°. CSmH, MH.

701 - The triumphs of London. J. and H. Playford, 1683. 4°. CSmH, ICU.

702 - The walks of Islington and Hogsdon, with The humours of Woodstreet-Compter. T. Wilson, 1657. 4°. (P 566) CSmH, DFo, DLC, ICN, ICU, MH.

703 - - [Anr.issue with cancel title.] Tricks of youth; or, The walks of Islington and Hogsdon, with The humours of Woodstreet-Compter. Printed by authority for the use of the author. 4°. CSmH, DFo.

>In some copies, the date 1663 is stamped below the imprint. See P 566, notes.

704 JOYNER, WILLIAM

>The Roman empress. T. N. for H. Herringman, 1671. 4°. CLUC, CSmH, CtY, DFo, DLC, ICN, ICU, MH, MWiW-C, MiU, NjP, TxU.

705 KILLIGREW, HENRY

>Pallantus and Eudora. J. Hardesty, 1653. fol. CSmII, DFo, DLC, MH.

706 - - [Anr.issue.] Printed in the year 1653. fol. (P 570) MH.

707 KILLIGREW, THOMAS

>Comedies and tragedies; [The princesse; or, Love at first sight; The parsons wedding; The pilgrim; Cicilia & Clorinda; or, Love in arms (2 parts); Thomaso; or, The wanderer (2 parts): Bellamira her dream; or, The love of shadows (2 parts); Claricilla; The prisoners.] H. Herringman, 1664. fol. (P 571) CLUC, CSmH, CtY, DLC, ICN, ICU, MH, MWiW-C, MiU, NIC, NjP, PU, TxU.

>>*Claricilla* and *The prisoners* have imprint: J. M. for A. Crook, 1663.

708 - - [Anr.issue.] DFo.

>>*Claricilla* and *The prisoners* have cancel title-page with imprint: J.M. for H.Herringman, 1664.

>- Claracilla. 1641. In his *The prisoners and Claracilla.*

709 - The prisoners and Claracilla. T. Cotes for A. Crooke, 1641. 12 mo. CLUC, CSmH, DFo, ICN, MH, MWiW-C, PU.

710 KILLIGREW, SIR WILLIAM
    Three playes: Selindra; Pandora; Ormasdes. T. Mabb for
    J. Playfere and T. Horsman, 1665. 8°. (P 573) CLUC,
    CSmH, DFo, DLC, ICN, MH, NjP, TxU.

711 - - [Anr.issue, with changed title.] Three new playes: Selindra;
    Ormasdes; Pandora. S. Neale, 1674. 8°. (P 573) CSmH,
    DFo, MH, MiU.
        Re-issue of unsold copies of 1665 edn. with a cancel title.

712 - Four new playes, viz: The seege of Urbin. Selindra. Love and
    friendship. Pandora. Oxford: H.Hall for R.Davis,1666.
    fol. (P 572) CLUC, CSmH, CtY, DFo, ICN, ICU, IEN,
    MH, MWiW-C, MiU, (first 2 plays only), NIC, NN, NjP,
    PU, TxU.

713 - The imperial tragedy. W. Wells and R. Scott, 1669. fol.
    CSmH, CtY, DFo, DLC, ICN, MH.
        Usually bound with *Four new playes*, 1666. CSmH also
        has copy with variant title-page.

    KIRKMAN, FRANCIS
    The merry conceited humours of Bottom the weaver. See
    under title.

    - The wits. See under title.

714 KNAVERY IN ALL TRADES; or, The coffee-house. J. B.
    for W. Gilbertson and H. Marsh, 1664. 4°. CSmH, DLC,
    MH.

715 LACY, JOHN
    The dumb lady; or, The farriar made physician. T. Dring,
    1672. 4°. CLUC, CSmH, CtY, DFo, DLC, ICN, MH,
    MiU, TxU.

716 - Sir Hercules Buffoon; or, The poetical squire. J. Hindmarsh,
    1684. 4°. CSmH, CtY, DFo, DLC, ICU, MH, MWiW-C,
    MiU.

LACY, JOHN (continued)

717   The old troop; or, Monsieur Raggou. W. Crook and T. Dring, 1672. 4°. CLUC, CSmH, CtY, DFo, ICN, ICU, MH, MiU.

718 - - [Anr.edn.] B. Tooke, 1698. 4°. CSmH, CtY, DFo, DLC, ICN, MH, NIC, NjP.

719 - Sauny the Scott; or, The taming of the shrew. E. Whitlock, 1698. 4°. CLUC, CSmH, CtY, DFo, ICU, MH, MiU, PU, TxU.

LADY ALIMONY; or, The alimony lady. 1659. See Greene, R. and T. Lodge.

720 LEANERD, JOHN

The counterfeits. J. Tonson, 1679. 4°. CSmH, CtY, DFo, DLC, ICN, ICU, MH, MiU, NjP, PU, TxU.

721 - The country innocence; or, The chamber-maid turn'd Quaker. C. Harper, 1677. 4°. (P 586) CSmH, CtY, DFo, DLC, ICN, MiU,

722 - The rambling justice; or, The jealous husbands. E. F. for T. Orrell and J. Vade, 1678. 4°. *CLUC, CSmH, DFo, MH.
Author's name on title-page.

723 - - [Anr.issue.] DFo, DLC, ICU, MWiW-C, MiU.
Author's name omitted from title. P 587 calls this another state of the title-page.

724 - - [Anr.issue, with changed title.] The jealous husbands . . . with The humours of Sir John Twiford and the rambling justice. T. Newman, 1680. 4°. CSmH. ICN.

725 - - [Anr.issue, with original title.] T. Bennet, 1694. 4°. DFo.
Only the type of gathering A is reset.

726 LEE, NATHANIEL

The works. R. Bentley, 1694. 2 vols. 4°. CtY.
General title-page struck off for a nonce collection of Lee's plays.

727 Caesar Borgia, son of Pope Alexander the sixth. 1679. (CBEL II, 412)

728 - - [Anr.edn.] R. E. for R. Bentley and M. Magnes, 1680. 4°. (M 114a) CLUC, CSmH, CtY, DFo, DLC, ICN, ICU, MH, MWiW-C, MiU, NjP, TxU.

729 - - [Anr.edn.] R. Bentley, 1696. 4°. (M 114b) DFo, ICU, **MH, TxU.**

730 - Constantine the great. H. Hills jun. for R. Bently and J. Tonson, 1684. 4°. (M 120) CLUC, CSmH, CtY, DFo, DLC, ICN, ICU, MH, MWiW-C, MiU, NjP, TxU.

- The Duke of Guise. See Dryden, J.

731 - Gloriana; or, The court of Augustus Caesar. J. Magnes and R. Bentley, 1676. 4°. (P 589) CLUC, CSmH, CtY, DFo, DLC, ICN, ICU, MH, MWiW-C, MiU, TxU.

732 - -[Anr.edn.] R. Wellington and E. Rumball, 1699. 4°. CtY, DFo, MH, TxU.

733 - Lucius Junius Brutus, father of his country. R. Tonson and J. Tonson, 1681. 4°. (P 590) CLUC, CSmH, CtY, DFo, DLC, ICN, ICU, MH, MWiW-C, MiU, NjP, PU, TxU.

734 - The massacre of Paris. R. Bentley and M. Magnes, 1690. 4°. (P 591) CLUC, CSmH, CtY, DFo, DLC, ICN, ICU, MH, MWiW-C, MiU, NIC, NjP, TxU.
    Pforzheimer calls this edition the first but CBEL lists a **1689 edition.**

735 - Mithridates King of Pontus. R. E. for J. Magnes and R. Bentley, 1678. 4°. (M 112a) CLUC, CSmH, CtY, DFo, DLC, ICN, ICU, MH, MWiW-C, NIC, NjP, TxU.

736 - - [Anr.edn.] R. E. for R. Bentley and S. Magnes, 1685. 4°. (M 112b) CLUC, DFo, MH, TxU.

LEE, NATHANIEL (continued)

737 - - [Anr.issue.]   R. E. for R. Bentley, 1685.   4°.   (Not in M)
   CSmH.

738 - - [Anr.edn.]   R. Bentley, 1693.   4°.   (M 112c)   CSmH, CtY,
   DFo, MH, MiU, TxU.

739 - - [Anr.edn.]   1697.   4°.   (CBEL II, 412 : M 112d)

   - Oedipus.   See Dryden, J.

   - Piso's conspiracy.   See under title.

740 - The princess of Cleve.   A. Roper, 1689.   4°.   CLUC, CSmH,
   CtY, DLC, ICN, ICU, MH, MWiW-C, TxU.

741 - - [Anr.edn.]   J. O. for R. Wellington, 1697.   4°.   CSmH,
   CtY, DFo, ICU, MH, TxU.

742 - The rival queens; or, The death of Alexander the great.   J.
   Magnes and R. Bentley, 1677.   4°.   (P 592 ; M 10a)   CLUC,
   CSmH, CtY, DFo, DLC, ICN, ICU, MH, MWiW-C, NjP,
   TxU.

743 - - [Anr.edn.]   J. Gain for R. Bentley, 1684.   4°.   (M 10b)
   CLUC, CSmH, CtY, DFo, ICN, ICU, MH, TxU.

744 - - [Anr.edn.]   R. Bentley, 1690.   4°.   CSmH, CtY, DFo, ICU,
   MH, TxU.

745 - - [Anr.edn.]   1691.   (CBEL II, 412)

746 - - [Anr.edn.]   R. Bentley, 1694.   4°.   (M 10c)   CSmH, CtY,
   DFo, ICN, ICU, MH, MiU, PU, TxU.
   "The second edition."

747 - - [Anr.edn.]   R. Wellington and E. Rumbal, 1699.   4°.   (M 10d)
   CSmH, DFo, MH.

748 - Sophinisba; or, Hannibal's overthrow.   1675.   (CBEL II, 412)

749 - - [Anr.edn.] J. Magnes and R. Bentley, 1676. 4°. CLUC, CSmH, CtY, DFo, DLC, ICN, ICU, MH, MWiW-C, NIC, **TxU.**

750 - - [Anr.edn.] R. Bently and M. Magnes, 1681. 4°. (M 117a) CLUC, CtY, DFo, DLC, ICU, MH.

751 - - [Anr.edn.] R. Bently and S. Magnes, 1685. 4°. (M 117b) CLUC, CSmH, CtY, DFo, TxU.

752 - - [Anr.edn.] R. Bently, 1691. 4°. (M 117c) CLUC.

753 - - [Anr.issue.] S. Briscoe, 1691. 4°. CSmH, ICU, TxU.

754 - - [Anr.edn.] T. Chapman, 1693. 4°. (M 117d) CLUC, CSmH, CtY, DFo, MH, TxU.

755 - - [Anr.edn.] 1697. 4°. (M 117e) CtY, DFo, MH, MiU, **TxU.**

756 - Theodosius; or, The force of love. R. Bentley and M. Magnes, 1680. 4°. (D and M 54) CSmH, DFo, DLC, ICU, MH (lacks songs), TxU.
Lacks advertisements on I4v.

757 - - [Anr.issue.] CLUC, CSmH, CtY, MH, NN, NjP, (imperfect).
Has advertisements on I4v.

758 - - [Anr.edn.] R. Bentley and S. Magnes, 1684. 4°. CLUC, CSmH, CtY, DFo, ICU, MiU, TxU.

759 - - [Anr.edn.] T. Chapman, 1692. 4°. CSmH, CtY, DFo, ICN, ICU, NjP, TxU.

760 - - [Anr.edn.] R. Bentley, 1697. 4°. CtY, DFo, MH, MiU.

LEE, NATHANIEL (continued)

761   The tragedy of Nero emperour of Rome. T. R. and N. T. for J. Magnus and R. Bentley, 1675. 4°. (P 593) CLUC, CSmH, CtY, DFo, DLC, ICN, ICU, MH, MWiW-C, MiU, **NjP, TxU.**

762 - - [Anr.edn.] R. Bentley, 1696. 4°. CtY, DFo, MH (2 variant copies), MiU.

763 LESLY, GEORGE
Divine dialogues. Viz. Dives's doom. Sodom's flames, and Abraham's faith. N. Woolfe, 1684. 8°. CSmH, DFo, MH. "Second edition." There is no trace of a first edition of about 1676, the date of the two dedications in the volume.

LODGE, THOMAS. See Greene, R. and T. Lodge.

764 THE LONDON CHAUNTICLERES. S. Miller, 1659. 4°. CSmH, CtY, DFo, DLC.

LOVE LOST IN THE DARK. See *The muse of New-market.*

765 LOVE WITHOUT INTEREST; or, The man too hard for the master. A. Bettesworth and R. Ellison, 1699. 4°. CSmH, DFo, DLC, MH, MiU, TxU.

766 LOWER, SIR WILLIAM
Three new playes: The noble ingratitude, The enchanted lovers, The amorous fantasme. F. Kirkman, 1661. 12°. CSmH, DLC, ICU.
The general title-page was inserted by the publisher, who frequently supplied cancel titles to the independent editions of the three plays here collected.

767 - The amourous fantasme. The Hague: J. Ramzey, 1660. 12°. CLUC, CSmH, DFo, ICU.
Translation from Quinault. Also found with this title-page in his *Three new playes,* 1661.

LOWER, SIR WILLIAM (continued)

768   The enchanted lovers. The Hague: Adrian Vlack, 1658. 12°.
CLUC, CSmH, CtY, DFo, ICU.
Also found with this title-page in his *Three new playes,*
1661.

769 - Horatius: a Roman tragedy. G. Bedell and T. Collins, 1656.
4°. CLUC, CSmH, DFo, DLC, ICN, ICU, MH.
Translated from P. Corneille.

770 - The noble ingratitude. The Hague: J. Ramzey, 1659. 12°.
CLUC, CSmH, DFo, ICU.
Also found with this title-page in his *Three new playes,*
1661.

771 - Polyeuctes; or, The martyr. T. Roycroft for G. Bedell and T.
Collins, 1655. 4°. CLUC, CSmH, DFo, ICN, MH, MWiW-C,
PU.
Translated from P. Corneille.

M., W.   See *The female wits.*

M., W.   See *The Huntingdon divertisement.*

772 MAIDWELL, LEWIS
The loving enemies. J. Guy, 1680. 4°. CSmH, CtY, DFo,
DLC, ICN, ICU, MH, MiU, TxU.
Erroneously attributed to Lawrence Maidwell.

773 THE MALL; or, The modish lovers. W. Cademan, 1674. 4°.
(M 144) CLUC, CSmH, CtY, DFo, DLC, ICN, ICU, MH,
MWiW-C, NN.

774 MANLEY, MARY DE LA RIVIERE
The lost lover; or, The jealous husband. R. Bently, F. Saun-
ders, J. Knapton, and R. Wellington, 1696. 4°. (P 637)
CLUC, CSmH, CtY, DLC, ICN, ICU, MH, MWiW-C,
MiU, NjP, TxU.

MANLEY, MARY DE LA RIVIERE (continued)

775 The royal mischief. R. Bentley, F. Saunders, and J. Knapton, 1696. 4°. CLUC, CSmH, CtY, DFo, DLC, ICN, ICU, MH, MWiW-C, MiU, NjP, TxU.

776 MANNING, FRANCIS
The generous choice. R. Wellington and A. Bettesworth, 1700. 4°. CSmH, DFo, DLC, ICN, MH, MWiW-C, MiU, NjP, TxU.

777 MANUCHE, COSMO
The bastard. M. M., T. Collins, and G. Bedell, 1652. 4° CLUC, CSmH, CtY, DFo, DLC, MH, MWiW-C.

778 The just general. M. M., T. C., and G. Bedell, 1652. 4°. (P 638) CSmH, DFo, ICN, MH.

779 - The loyal lovers. T. Eglesfield, 1652. 4°. CSmH, DFo, DLC, ICU, MH, TxU.

780 MARLOWE, CHRISTOPHER
Lusts dominion; or, The lascivious queen. F. K. and sold by R. Pollard, 1657. 12°. DLC.
Author's name omitted from title. Frequently attributed to Dekker, Haughton, and Day.

781 - - [Anr.issue.] (P 644) CSmH, MH.
The issue with author's name on title.

782 - - [Anr.issue, with paste-on cancel imprint.] T. J. and sold by R. P. and W. Wright, 1658. 12°.
See P 644, notes.

783 - - [Anr.issue, with paste-on cancel imprint.] F. Kirkman, 1661. 12°. DLC.
See P 644, notes.

784 Entry cancelled.

785 MARMION, SHACKERLEY
    The antiquary. F. K. for J. W. and F. E., 1641. 4°. CLUC, CSmH, CtY, DFo, DLC, ICN, ICU, MH, MWiW-C, NjP, PU, TxU.

    THE MARRIAGE BROAKER; or, The pander. 1662. In *Gratiae theatrales.* 1662.

786 MARSTON, JOHN
    Comedies, tragi-comedies, & tragedies. Printed Ann: Dom: 1652. 4°. CSmH.
        A general title-page printed for a nonce collection of early quartos, now broken up and dispersed. See P 658, notes.

787 MASON, JOHN
    Princeps rhetoricus; or, Pilomachia, The combat of caps. H.R.,1648. 4°. DFo.

    - The school moderator. See his *Princeps rhetoricus.*

788 MASSINGER, PHILIP
    Three new playes; viz. The bashful lover, Guardian, Very woman. H. Moseley, 1655. 8°. (P 681) CLUC, CSmH, CtY, DFo, DLC, ICN, MH, MWiW-C, NIC (lacks Very woman), NjP, TxU.

    - The bashful lover. 1655. In his *Three new playes,* 1655.

789 - The city-madam. A. Pennycuicke one of the actors, 1658. 4°. CSmH, ICU, NjP.

790 - - [Anr.issue.] A. Pennycuicke one of the actors, 1659. 4°. CLUC, CSmH, CtY, DFo, DLC, MH, MiU, TxU.
        Pennycuicke dedicated his play to at least four different patrons: 1. John Wroth, ICU copy; 2. Mr. Lee, ICU copy; 3. Thomas Freake, Bodley copy; 4. Lady Ann, Countess of Oxford, British Museum copies. Apparently all copies dated 1659 and a few dated 1658 are dedicated to the Countess of Oxford.

MASSINGER, PHILIP (continued)
  The guardian. 1655. In his *Three new playes,* 1655.

- A very woman. 1655. In his *Three new playes,* 1655.

791 MASSINGER, PHILIP and THOMAS DEKKER
  The virgin-martyr. B.A.,1651. 4°. (P 683) CLUC, CSmH,
  DFo, ICN, MH.

792 - - [Anr.edn.] W. Sheares, 1661. 4°. CSmH, CtY, DFo,
  DLC, ICN, MH.

793 MASSINGER, PHILIP, THOMAS MIDDLETON, and
  WILLIAM ROWLEY
  The excellent comedy, called The old law; or, A new way to
  please you. E. Archer, 1656. 4°. CSmH, CtY, DFo, ICN,
  ICU, MH, MWiW-C, NjP, TxU.

794 MAY, THOMAS
  Two tragedies: viz. Cleopatra queene of AEgypt. And Agrip-
  pina empress of Rome. H.Moseley,1654. 12°. CSmH,
  DFo, DLC (Cleopatra only), NjP, PU.
  A re-issue of the edition of 1639, with a general title and
  cancel titles for *Agrippina* and *Cleopatra.*

795 - The old couple. J. Cottrel for S. Speed, 1658. 4°. (P 685)
  CLUC, CSmH, CtY, DFo, DLC, ICN, ICU, MH, MWiW-C,
  PU, TxU.

- The tragedy of Cleopatra queen of Egypt. 1654. In his *Two
  tragedies,* 1654.

- The tragedy of Julia Agrippina empress of Rome. 1654. In
  his *Two tragedies,* 1654.

796 MAYNE, JASPER
  Two plaies. The city match. And The amorous warre. Ox-
  ford. Re-printed by Hen.Hall, for Rich Davis,1658. 4°.
  CSmH (City match only), DFo, MII (City match only.)

The general title, plus *City match*, signed A-I⁴ without special title, plus unsigned leaf of epilogue; and 1648 edition of *Amorous warre*, signed A-L⁴.

797 - - [Anr.issue.] TxU (Amorous warre only).
As above, except that *Amorous warre* has a paste-on cancel imprint, "Oxford, Printed for Ric. Davis. 1658."

798 - - [Anr.issue or edn.] *DFo (Amorous warre only), ICU (Amorous warre only), *PU (Amorous warre only).
As above except that *Amorous warre* is a reprint, with the imprint, "Oxford, Printed by Henry Hall Printer to the University, for Ric. Davis, 1659." L4 is blank.

799 - - [Anr.issue.]
As above, but *Amorous warre*, 1659, has on L4 a Catalogue of books, some dated 1662.

800 - The amorous warre. Printed in the yeare 1648. 4°. CLUC, CSmH, CtY, DFo, DLC, MWiW-C, NjP, TxU.
Also included in the first issue of his *Two plaies*, 1658.

801 - - [Anr.edn.] Oxford, Printed by Henry Hall for Ric. Davis, 1659. 8°. CSmH, CtY, DFo, DLC, ICN, MH, MiU.
The octavo edition is signed A-F⁸.

- The city match. 1658. In his *Two plaies*, 1658.

802 - - [Anr.edn.] Oxford, Printed by Henry Hall, for Rich: Davis, 1659. 8°. DFo, ICN, ICU, MiU.
The octavo edition is signed A-E⁸.

803 MEAD, ROBERT
The combat of love and friendship. M. M., G. Bedell, and T. Collins, 1654. 4°. CLUC, CSmH, CtY, DFo, DLC, ICN, MH, MWiW-C, NIC, NjP, PU.

804 MEDBOURNE, MATTHEW
Saint Cecily; or, The converted twins. J. Streator, 1666. 4°. CSmH, DFo, DLC, ICN.

MEDBOURNE, MATTHEW (continued)

805 - - [Anr.edn. with changed title.] The converted twins. R. Pawlett, 1667. 4°. CLUC, CSmH, MH.

806 - Tartuffe; or, The French Puritan. H. L. and R. B. for J. Magnus, 1670. 4°. CSmH, DFo, DLC, MH, MWiW-C, NIC, NN.

MENDOZA, ANTONIO DE
Querer por solo querer. See Fanshawe, Sir R.

807 MERITON, THOMAS
Love and war. C. Webb, 1658. 4°. CSmH, CtY, DFo, DLC, ICN, ICU, MH, MWiW-C, PU.

808 - The wandring lover. T. L. for T. C. and W. Burden, 1658. 4°. CLUC, CSmH, DFo, DLC, ICU, MWiW-C.

809 THE MERRY CONCEITED HUMORS OF BOTTOM THE WEAVER. F. Kirkman and H. Marsh, 1661. 4°. CSmH, DFo, MH.

810 THE MERRY DEVIL OF EDMONTON. W. Gilbertson, 1655. 4°. (G 264f) CSmH, DFo.

811 A MERRY DIALOGUE BETWEEN BAND, CUFF, AND RUFF. F. K., 1661. 4°. (G 326c) CSmH, DLC, MH.

THE MERRY MILKMAID OF ISLINGTON; or, The rambling gallants defeated. See *The muse of New-Market.* 1680.

812 MIDDLETON, THOMAS
Two new playes. Viz.: More dissemblers besides women. Women beware women. H. Moseley, 1657. 8°. CSmH, CtY, DFo, DLC, ICN, MH, MWiW-C, NjP, TxU.

813 - Any thing for a quiet life. T. Johnson for F. Kirkman and H. Marsh, 1662. 4°. CSmH, DFo, DLC, ICU, MH, MWiW-C.

MIDDLETON, THOMAS (continued)

The counterfeit bridegroom; or, The defeated widow. See
Behn, A.

- The excellent comedie, called The old law. See Massinger, P.,
T. Middleton, and W. Rowley.

814 - The mayor of Quinborough: a comedy. H. Herringman, 1661.
4°. (P 697) CSmH, CtY, DFo, DLC, ICN, ICU, MH,
MWiW-C, NjP, PU, TxU.
CSmH has a variant with "Tragedy" in line 6 of title-page.

- More dissemblers besides women. 1657. In his *Two new
playes,* 1657.

815 - No wit no help like a womans. H. Moseley, 1657. 8°. (P 700)
CLUC, CSmH, CtY, DFo, DLC, ICN, ICU, MH, MWiW-C,
NjP, PU.

816 - The Spanish gipsie. J. G. for R. Marriot, 1653. 4°. CSmH,
CtY, DFo, ICN, ICU, MH.

817 - - [Anr.edn.] T. C. and L. P. for R. Crofts, 1661. 4°. CSmH,
CtY, DFo, DLC, ICN, MH, MjP.

818 - - [Anr.issue.] T. C. and L. P. for F. Kirkman, 1661. 4°.
CSmH, DLC.

-Women beware women. 1657. In his *Two new playes,* 1657.

819 MIDDLETON, THOMAS and WILLIAM ROWLEY
The changeling. H. Moseley, 1653. 4°. (P 691) CSmH,
CtY, DFo, *DLC, MH, MWiW-C, NN, PU, TxU.

820 - - [Anr.issue.] Printed in the year, 1653. 4°. CSmH.

821 - - [Anr.issue.] A. M. sold by T. Dring, 1668. 4°. CSmH,
ICN, MH.

822 MILTON, JOHN

Arcades. 1645. 8° In his *Poems of Mr. John Milton.* R. Raworth for H. Moseley, 1645. (P 722) CLUC, CSmH, CtY, DFo, ICN, MH, NN, NjP, TxU.

823 - - [Anr.edn.] 1673. 8°. In his *Poems.* T. Dring at the White Lion, 1673. (P 723) CSmH, CtY, DFo, MH, MiU, NIC, NN, TxU.

824 - - [Anr.issue.] In his *Poems.* T. Dring at the Blew Anchor, 1673. (P 724) CLUC, CSmH, ICN, ICU, MH, NN, NjP.

825 - - [Anr.edn.] 1695. fol. In his *The poetical works.* J. Tonson, 1695. CLUC, CSmH, CtY, DLC, ICN, ICU, MH, NN, NjP, TxU.

- Comus. See his *A mask ... presented at Ludlow-Castle,* 1634.

826 - A mask ... presented at Ludlow-Castle, 1634. Anno. Dom. 1645. 8°. In his *Poems.* R. Raworth for H. Moseley, 1645. (P 722) CLUC, CSmH, CtY, DFo, ICN, MH, NN, NjP, TxU.

827 - - [Anr.edn.] 1673. In his *Poems.* T. Dring at the White Lion, 1673. (P 723) CSmH, CtY, DFo, MH, MiU, NIC, NN, TxU.

828 - - [Anr.issue.] In his *Poems.* T. Dring at the Blew Anchor, 1673. (P 724) CLUC, CSmH, ICN, ICU, MH, NN, NjP.

829 - - [Anr.edn.] 1695. fol. In his *The poetical works.* J. Tonson, 1695. CLUC, CSmH, CtY, DLC, ICN, ICU, MH, NN, NjP, TxU.

830 - Samson Agonistes. J. M. for J. Starkey, 1671. 8°. In his *Paradise regained,* 1671. CLUC, CSmH, CtY, ICN, MH, MWiW-C, MiU, NN, NjP, TxU.

831 - - [Anr.edn.] J. Starkey, 1680. 8°. In his *Paradise regained,* 1680. CLUC, CSmH, CtY, DFo, ICN, ICU, MH, MWiW-C, MiU, NIC, NN, NjP, TxU.

MILTON, JOHN (continued)

832 - - [Anr.edn.] R. Taylor, 1688. fol. (P 721) In his *Paradise regained*. 1688. CSmH, CtY, ICN, ICU, MH, NIC, NN, PU, TxU.

833 - - [Anr.edn.] R. E., sold by J. Whitlock, 1695. fol. In his *Poetical works*. 1695. CSmH, DLC, NjP.

834 THE MISTAKEN BEAUTY; or, The lyar. S. Neale, 1685. 4°. CSmH, CtY, DFo, DLC, MiU.
 Translated from P. Corneille.

835 THE MISTAKEN HUSBAND. J. Magnes and R. Bentley, 1675. 4°. (M 145; P 333) CSmH, CtY, DFo, DLC, ICN, ICU, MH, MWiW-C, TxU.

836 MR. TURBULENT; or, The melanchollicks. S. Neale, 1682. 4°. Bodley.

837 - - [Anr.issue, with changed title.] The factious citizen; or, The melancholy visioner. T. Maddocks, 1685. 4°. CSmH, DFo, DLC, ICN, MiU.

838 MONTAGU, WALTER
 The shepheard's paradise. T. Dring, 1629 [i.e. 1659.] 8°. CSmH, DFo, MH, MWiW-C.

839 - - [Anr.issue.] J. Starkey, 1659. 8°. CSmH, DFo, DLC, ICN, ICU, MH.

840 A MOST PLEASANT COMEDY OF MUCEDORUS THE KINGS SON OF VALENTIA, AND AMADINE THE KINGS DAUGHTER OF ARAGON. WITH THE MERRY CONCEITS OF MOUSE. F. Coles, [post 1656.] 4°. (G 151o) CSmH, DFo.

841 - - [Anr.edn.] F. Coles, 1663. 4°. (G 151p) Boston Public Library.

842 - - [Anr.edn.] E. O. for F. Coles, 1668. 4°. (G 151q) CSmH, DFo, NN.

843 MOTTEUX, PETER ANTHONY
  Beauty in distress. D. Brown and R. Parker, 1698. 4°. CLUC, CSmH, DFo, DLC, ICN, ICU, MH, MWiW-C, TxU.

844 Europes revels for the peace; and His Majesties happy return. J. Tonson, 1697. 4°. ICU.

845 - The four seasons; or, Love in every age. R. Wellington, sold by B. Lintott, 1699. 4°. CSmH, DFo, ICU.
  Printed at end of *The island princess.*

846 - The island princess; or, The generous Portuguese. R. Wellington, sold by B. Lintott, 1699. 4°. CLUC, CSmH, DFo, DLC, ICU, MH, NIC, NjP.

847 - Love's a jest. P. Buck, J. Sturton, and A. Bosvil, 1696. 4°. (P 746) CLUC, CSmH, CtY, DFo, DLC, ICN, ICU, MH, MWiW-C, MiU, NN, NjP, TxU.

848 - The loves of Mars and Venus. Printed and are to be sold at the New Theatre in Little-Lincolns-Inn-fields, 1696. 4°. CLUC, CSmH, DFo.

849 - - [Anr.issue.] 1697. 4°. CSmH, DFo, ICN, ICU, MH, MWiW-C, MiU, NN, TxU.
  Sometimes bound with Ravenscroft's *The anatomist.*

850 - The novelty; Every act a play. R. Parker and P. Buck, 1697. 4°. CLUC, CSmH, CtY, DFo, DLC, ICN, ICU, MH, MiU, NIC, NjP, TxU.
  Includes *Thyrsis* by John Oldmixon and *The unfortunate couple* by Edward Filmer.

851 MOUNTFORT, WILLIAM
  Greenwich-Park. J. Hindmarsh, R. Bentley, and A. Roper, sold by R. Taylor, 1691. 4°. CLUC, CSmH, DFo, DLC, ICN, MH, MWiW-C, NjP, TxU.

  - Henry the second. See Bancroft, J.

MOUNTFORT, WILLIAM (continued)
852　The injur'd lovers; or, The ambitious father.　S. Manship,
　　　 1688.　4°.　CSmH, CtY, DFo, DLC, ICN, ICU, MH,
　　　 MWiW-C, NjP, TxU.

- King Edward the third.　See Bancroft, J.

853 - The life and death of Doctor Faustus... with the humours of
　　　 Harlequin and Scaramouche.　E. Whitlock, 1697.　4°.　CSmH,
　　　 DFo, ICN, MH.

854　The successfull straingers.　J. Blackwell, sold by R. Taylor,
　　　 1690.　4°.　CLUC, CSmH, CtY, DFo, DLC, ICN.

855 - - [Anr.issue.]　W. Freeman, 1696.　4°.　CtY, DFo, DLC, ICU,
　　　 MH, NjP.

MUCEDORUS.　See *A most pleasant comedy of Mucedorus*.

856 THE MUSE OF NEW-MARKET; or, Mirth and drollery,
　　　 being three farces... viz: The merry milkmaid of Islington;
　　　 or, The rambling gallants defeated; Love lost in the dark; or,
　　　 The drunken couple; The politick whore; or, The conceited
　　　 cuckold.　D. Browne, D. Major, and J. Vade, 1680.　4°.
　　　 CSmH, DFo (part 3 only), DLC, MH.

857 MUSIC; or, A parley of instruments.　The first part.　Printed
　　　 in the year, 1676.　4°.　CSmH.

NEGLECTED VIRTUE.　See Hopkins, C.

858 NEVILE, ROBERT
　　　 The poor scholar.　T. Johnson for F. Kirkman and H. Marsh,
　　　 1662.　4°.　CLUC, CSmH, CtY, DFo, DLC, ICU, MWiW-C,
　　　 MiU.

859 NEWES OUT OF THE WEST; or, The character of a mounte-
　　　 bank.　Printed in the yeare of Grace, 1647.　4°.　CSmH.

860 NORTON, RICHARD
Pausanias the betrayer of his country. A. Roper, E. Wilkinson, and R. Clavell, 1696. 4°. CSmH, CtY, DFo, DLC, ICN, ICU, MH, MiU, NjP.

861 OGILBY, JOHN
The relation of his Majestie's entertainment passing through the city of London. T.Roycroft for R.Marriott,1661. fol. DFo.

862 - - [Anr.edn.] Re-printed at Edinburgh, 1661. 4°. ICN.

863 - The entertainment of his most excellent Majestie Charles II in his passage through the city of London to his coronation. T. Roycroft, 1662. fol. ICN.

864 - - [Anr.edn.] Wm. Morgan, 1685. fol.

865 OLDMIXON, JOHN
Amintas. R. Parker, 1698. 4°. CLUC, CSmH, DFo, DLC, ICU, MH, MiU, TxU.
Translated from T. Tasso.

866 - The grove; or, Love's paradice. R. Parker, 1700. 4°. CLUC, CSmH, CtY, DFo, DLC, ICN, MH, MWiW-C, MiU, NjP, TxU.

- Thyrsis. See Motteux, P. A. *The novelty.*

867 OTWAY, THOMAS
Works. R. Bentley, 1691. 4°. ICU.
General title-page of nonce collection of plays. Two plays dated after 1691.

868 - - [Anr.edn.] R. Bentley, 1692. 4°. TxU.
General title-page of nonce collection of plays.

869 - Alcibiades. W. Cademan, 1675. 4°. *CSmH, *CtY, *DLC, ICN, *MH, *MWiW-C, *PU.
Running-titles in type of two different sizes; text in type of two sizes.

OTWAY, THOMAS (continued)

870 - - [Anr.edn.]   1675.   4°.
> Type of uniform size in text and running-titles.

871 - - [Anr.edn.]   R. Bentley and S. Magnes, 1687.   4°.   CLUC,
CSmH, CtY, DFo, DLC, ICU, MH, MWiW-C, MiU, NjP,
PU, TxU.

872 - The atheist; or, The second part of The souldiers fortune.   R.
Bentley and J. Tonson, 1684.   4°.   CLUC, CSmH, CtY, DFo,
DLC, ICN, ICU, MH, MWiW-C, MiU, NIC, NjP, TxU.

- The cheats of Scapin.   See his *Titus and Berenice*.

873 - Don Carlos Prince of Spain.   R. Tonson, 1676.   4°.   CSmH,
CtY, DFo, MH, NjP, TxU.

874 - - [Anr.edn.]   E.Flesher for R.Tonson,1679.   4°.   CSmH,
CtY, DFo, ICU, MH, TxU.

875 - - [Anr.edn.]   R. Tonson, 1686.   4°.   CSmH, CtY, DFo, DLC,
ICN, ICU, MH, TxU.

876 - - [Anr.edn.]   R. Bentley, 1695.   4°.   CLUC, CtY, DFo, DLC,
MH, MiU, TxU.

877 - Friendship in fashion.   E. F. for R. Tonson, 1678.   4°.   (P 776)
CLUC, CSmH, *CtY, DFo, *DLC, ICN, ICU, MH,
*MWiW-C, *MiU, *NjP, *PU, TxU.
> The first state of the first issue, with line 11 of the title-
> page reading "Licenced May 31. 1678. Roger L'Estrange.";
> the first printing of the dedication, with two rules at top
> of A2, the catchword "Play," and on A2v the signature
> "Thomas Otway."

878 - - [Anr.issue.]   DFo.
> The text of the play is identical. Line 11 of the title has
> been altered to read "Licenced, &c." In the DFo copy, the
> dedication is printed from the same setting of type as be-
> fore, but the two rules at top of page A2 have been omitted,

and two lines of text have been borrowed from A2v, so that the catchword is "first;" the dedication is signed "T. O." See P 776.

879 - - [Anr.issue.] CSmH.
The title-page is printed from a different setting of type. Line 11 reads, "Licenced, May 31. Roger Le 'Estrange" [no period]. The dedication in the CSmH copy is like that in the DFo copy, No. 878. See P 776.

880 - The history and fall of Caius Marius. T. Flesher, 1680. 4°. CLUC, CSmH, CtY, DFo, ICN, ICU, MH, MiU, NIC, NjP, TxU.

881 - - [Anr.edn.] R.Bentley,1692. 4°. CSmH, DFo, DLC, MWiW-C, *PU.
Long "s" in quotation on title-page.

882 - - [Anr.issue.] CSmH, DFo, ICU.
Short "s" in quotation on title-page.

883 - - [Anr.issue.] T. Flesher, 1692. 4°. IEN.

884 - - [Anr.edn.] 1694. (Summers).

885 - - [Anr.edn.] R. Bentley, 1696. 4°. CSmH, DFo, DLC, MH, TxU.

886 - The orphan; or, The unhappy-marriage. R. Bentley and M. Magnes, 1680. 4°. CLUC, CSmH, CtY, DFo, DLC, ICN, MH, MWiW-C, NjP, TxU.

887 - - [Anr.edn.] R.Bentley and S.Magnes,1685. 4°. DFo, MH, NIC.

888 - - [Anr.edn.] R. Bentley, 1691. 4° CSmH, CtY, DFo, ICU, MH, MiU, NN, TxU.

889 - - [Anr.edn.] R. Bentley, 1696. 4°. CSmH, CtY, DFo, DLC, ICU, MH, TxU.

890 The souldiers fortune. R. Bentley and M. Magnes, 1681. 4°. (P 778) CLUC, CSmH, CtY, DFo, DLC, ICN, MH, MWiW-C, MiU.

891 - - [Anr.edn.] R.Bentley and S.Magnes,1683. 4°. CSmH, DFo, MH, NIC, TxU.

892 - - [Anr.edn.] R.Bentley and S.Magnes,1687. 4°. CLUC, CSmH, CtY, DFo, DLC, ICU, MH, TxU.

893 - - [Anr.edn.] R. Bentley, 1695. 4°. CtY, DFo, MH, TxU.

894 - Titus and Berenice ... with a farce called The cheats of Scapin. R. Tonson, 1677. 4°. CtY, DFo, ICU.
With 37 lines on p. 17.

895 - - [Anr.issue.] CLUC, CSmH, DFo, DLC, ICN, MH, MWiW-C, MiU, NjP, TxU.
P. 17 (C1) a cancel leaf with 41 lines instead of 37.

896 - Venice preserv'd; or, A plot discover'd. J. Hindmarsh, 1682. 4°. (P 779) CLUC, CSmH, CtY, DFo, DLC, ICN, ICU, MH, MWiW-C, MiU, NjP, PU, TxU.

897 - - [Anr.edn.] J. Knapton, 1696. 4°. CtY, DFo, DLC, MH, MiU, TxU.

898 - - [Anr.edn.] R. Bentley and J. Knapton, 1696. 4°. CtY, NN, TxU.

P., W. See *The converted fryar.*

899 PAYNE, HENRY NEVIL
The fatal jealousie. T. Dring, 1673. 4°. CLUC, CSmH, CtY, DFo, DLC, ICN, MH, MWiW-C, MiU.

900 - The morning ramble; or, The town-humours. T. Dring, 1673. 4°. CLUC, CSmH, CtY, DFo, DLC, ICN, MH, MWiW-C, MiU, NjP.

PAYNE, HENRY NEVIL (continued)

901 The siege of Constantinople. T. Dring, 1675. 4°. CLUC, CSmH, CtY, DFo, DLC, ICN, ICU, MH, MWiW-C, MiU, NjP, TxU.

902 PEAPS, WILLIAM
Love in it's extasie; or, The large prerogative. W. Wilson for M. Meighen, G. Bedell, and T. Collins, 1649. 4°. CSmH, CtY, DLC, ICU, MH.

903 PERRIN, PIERRE
Ariadne; or, The marriage of Bacchus. T. Newcombe, 1674. 4°. CSmH, DFo, NjP.

904 PHILIPS, KATHERINE
Horace. H. Herringman, 1667. fol. In her *Poems,* 1667. CLUC, CSmH, CtY, DFo, ICN, MH, MiU.
Translated from P. Corneille.

905 - - [Anr.edn.] J.M. for H.Herringman,1669. fol. In her *Poems,* 1669. CLUC, DFo, MH.

906 - - [Anr.edn.] T. N. for H. Herringman, 1678. fol. In her *Poems,* 1678. CLUC, CSmH, DFo, DLC, ICU, MH, MiU.

907 - Pompey. J. Crooke, 1663. 4°. CLUC, CSmH, CtY, DFo, MiU.
Translated from P. Corneille.

908 - - [Anr.edn.] Dublin: J. Crooke for S. Dancer, 1663. 4°. DFo, TxU.

909 - - [Anr.edn.] H. Herringman, 1664. 4°. DFo, TxU.
Summers lists a 1664 edn. in a pirated edn. of her poems dated 1664.

910 - - [Anr.edn.] H. Herringman, 1667. fol. In her *Poems,* 1667. CLUC, CSmH, CtY, DFo, ICN, MH, MiU.

PHILIPS, KATHERINE (continued)

911 - -[Anr.edn.] H. Herringman, 1669. fol. In her *Poems*, 1669.
CLUC, DFo, MH.

912 - - [Anr.edn.] H. Herringman, 1678. fol. In her *Poems,* 1678.
CLUC, CSmH, DFo, DLC, ICU, MH, MiU.

913 PHILIPS, WILLIAM
Alcamenes and Menalippa. [1668.] (Summers)

914 - The revengeful queen. P. Buck, 1698. 4°. CSmH, CtY,
DFo, DLC, ICN, ICU, MH, MWiW-C, MiU, NjP.

915 - St. Stephens-Green; or, The generous lovers. Dublin: J.
Brocas, 1700. 4°. CSmH.

PHILOPROTEST.
The converted fryar. See under title.

PINKETHMAN, WILLIAM
Love without interest. See under title.

916 PISO'S CONSPIRACY. T. M. for W. Cademan, 1676. 4°.
CLUC, CSmH, CtY, DFo, DLC, ICN, MH, NjP.

917 PIX, MARY
The beau defeated; or, The lucky younger brother. W. Turner and R. Basset, [1700.] CSmH, DLC, ICN, MiU.

918 - The deceiver deceived. R. Basset, 1698. 4°. CSmH, DFo,
DLC, ICN, ICU, MH.

919 - The false friend; or, The fate of disobedience. R. Basset,
1699. 4°. CSmH, CtY, DFo, DLC, ICN, ICU.

920 - Ibrahim the thirteenth Emperour of the Turks. J. Harding
and R. Wilkin, 1696. 4°. CSmH, CtY, DFo, DLC, ICN,
ICU, MH, MWiW-C, MiU, NjP, TxU.

PIX, MARY (continued)

921   The innocent mistress. J. Orme for R. Basset and F. Cogan, 1697. 4°. CSmH, CtY, TxU.
    "Near Temple-Bar in Fleetstreet," in imprint.

922 - - [Anr.issue.] CSmH, DFo, DLC, ICN, ICU, MH, MWiW-C, MiU, NjP, TxU.
    "At the Miter within Temple-Bar" in imprint; with errata at end of last page.

923 - Queen Catharine; or, The ruines of love. W.Turner and R. Basset, 1698. 4°. CLUC, CSmH, CtY, DFo, DLC, ICN, ICU, MH, MWiW-C, MiU, NjP, TxU.

924 - The Spanish wives. R. Wellington, 1696. 4°. CSmH, CtY, DFo, DLC, ICN, ICU, MH, MWiW-C, MiU, NjP, TxU.

PLAUTUS, TITUS MACCIUS
Comedies. See Echard, L.

925 A PLEASANT COMEDY CALLED THE TWO MERRY MILK-MAIDS. By J.C. T.Johnson, sold by N.Brook, F. Kirkman, T. Johnson, and H. Marsh, 1661. 4°. CSmH, CtY, DFo, DLC, ICN, ICU, MH, NIC.

926 A PLEASANT COMEDY, CALLED WILY BEGUILDE. W. Gilbertson, [c.1653.] 4°. (G 234g) CSmH, MH.

927 PLUTO FURENS ET VINCTUS; or, The raging devil bound. Amstelodami, in usum Theatri Amstelredemensis, 1669. 4°. CSmH, DFo, MH.

THE POLITICK WHORE. See *The muse of New-Market*.

928 PORDAGE, SAMUEL
    Herod and Mariamne. W. Cademan, 1673. 4°. CSmH, CtY, DFo, DLC, ICN, ICU, MWiW-C, MiU, TxU.

929 - - [Anr.issue.] W.Cademan,1674. 4°. CSmH, DFo, DLC, TxU.

PORDAGE, SAMUEL (continued)

930   The siege of Babylon. R. Tonson, 1678. 4°. (P 804) CLUC, CSmH, DFo, DLC, ICN, ICU, MH, MWiW-C, MiU, TxU.

- Troades Englished. 1660. See Seneca, L. A.

931 PORTER, THOMAS
     The carnival. H. Herringman, 1664. 4°. (P 806) CLUC, CSmH, DFo, DLC, ICN, ICU, MH, MWiW-C, MiU, NjP.

932 - The French conjurer. L. Curtis, 1678. 4°. CSmH, DFo, DLC, ICN, ICU, MH, MiU, NjP.

933 - The villain. H. Herringman and S. Speed, 1663. 4°. CLUC, CSmH, CtY, DFo, DLC, ICN, MH, MWiW-C, MiU.

934 - - [Anr.edn.] H.Herringman, 1670. 4°. CtY, DFo, DLC, ICN, ICU, MH, MiU, NN, TxU.

935 - - [Anr.edn.] T. Warren for H. Herringman, sold by R. Bentley, J. Tonson, F. Saunders, and T. Bennet, 1694. 4°. CSmH, DFo, MH, NIC, NjP, TxU.

936 - A witty combat; or, The female victor. T. Roberts, 1663. 4°. CSmH, CtY, DFo, DLC, ICN, ICU, MH.

937 POWELL, GEORGE
     Alphonso King of Naples. A. Roper and T. Bever, 1691. 4°. CLUC, CSmH, CtY, DFo, DLC, ICN, ICU, MH, MWiW-C, MiU, NjP, TxU.

938 - Bonduca; or, The British heroine. R. Bentley, 1696. 4°. CLUC, CSmH, DFo, DLC, ICN, MH, MiU, NjP, TxU.

- The Cornish comedy. See under title.

939 - The imposture defeated; or, A trick to cheat the devil. R. Wellington, 1698. 4°. CSmH, DFo, DLC, ICN, MH, MiU, NjP, TxU.

POWELL, GEORGE (continued)

940 A new opera called Brutus of Alba; or, Augusta's triumph.
W. Onley for S. Briscoe, 1697. 4°. CSmH, CtY, DFo,
DLC, ICN, ICU, MiU, NjP.
Written in collaboration with John Verbruggen.

941 - - [Anr.issue.] W. Onley for S. Briscoe, R. Welinton, and H.
Nelmes, 1697. 4°. MH, MWiW-C.

942 - The treacherous brothers. J. Blackwell, sold by R. Taylor,
1690. 4°. CSmH, CtY, DFo, ICN, ICU, MWiW-C, MiU,
NjP, TxU.

943 - - [Anr.issue.] W. Freeman, 1696. 4°. CSmH, DFo, DLC,
ICN, MH, TxU.

944 - - [Anr.edn.] 1699. (CBEL II, 426)

945 - A very good wife. S. Briscoe, 1693. 4°. CSmH, CtY, DFo,
DLC, ICN, ICU, MH, MWiW-C, MiU, NjP, TxU.

946 PRESTWICH, EDMUND
The hectors; or, The false challenge. G. Bedel and T. Collins,
1656. 4°. CSmH, DFo, ICN, ICU, MH, NIC, TxU.

- Hippolitus. See Seneca, L.A.

THE PRINCE OF PRIGGS REVELS. See S., J. *An excellent comedy, called, the prince of priggs revels.*

947 PURITANICAL JUSTICE; or, The beggars turned thieves.
J. Wells, 1698. 4°. CSmH.

948 QUARLES, FRANCIS
The virgin widow. R. Royston, 1649. 4°. CLUC, CSmH,
DFo, DLC, ICN, MH, MWiW-C, TxU.

949 - - [Anr.edn.] R. Royston, 1656. 4°. CSmH, DFo, ICN,
MH, PU.

950 THE QUEEN; or, The excellency of her sex. T. N. for T.
Heath, 1653. 4°. CSmH, CtY, DFo, ICU, MH.

QUINAULT, PHILIPPE
Agrippa King of Alba. See Dancer, J.

- The amorous fantasme. See Lower, W.

R., T.
The extravagant sheepherd. See under title.

R., W.
The Christmas ordinary. See under title.

RACINE, JEAN BAPTISTE
Achilles. See Boyer, A.

- Andromache. See Crowne, J.

- Bérénice. See Otway, T. *Titus and Berenice.*

951 THE RAMPANT ALDERMAN; or, News from the exchange.
R. Taylor, 1685. 4°. CSmH, CtY, DFo, DLC, ICU, MH,
TxU.

952 RANDOLPH, THOMAS
Poems, with The muses looking-glasse, and Amyntas. Whereunto is added, The jealous lovers. Printed in the Yeer 1643.
8°. CLUC, CtY, DFo, MH.
In this issue, *The muses looking-glasse* has separate title-
page with imprint, "Printed Anno Dom. 1643."; *Amyntas,*
separate title-page with imprint, "Oxford. L. Lichfield, for
Francis Bowman. 1640."; and *Jealous lovers,* title-page
with the Cambridge imprint, "Roger Daniel: 1640. Sold
by Richard Ireland."

953 - - [Anr.issue.] CSmH.
In this issue, *Jealous lovers* is a new edition, with imprint,
"London, for Richard Royston, 1646."

954 - - [Anr.edn., including for the first time *Arystippus*.] F. Bowman, sold by W. Roybould, 1652. 8°. (P 829) CSmH, DFo, DLC, ICN, ICU, MH, NN, TxU.
Each play has title-page, with imprint, "Printed in the Yeare. 1652."; except *The muses looking-glasse*, whose imprint is: "London. Printed Anno Dom. 1652."

955 - - [Anr.issue.] Printed in the Yeare, 1652. 8°. CLUC, CtY, DFo, MH, NN, NjP.

956 - - [Anr.edn.] F. Bowman, sold by T. Bowman, Bookseller in Oxford, 1664. 8°. DFo, DLC, ICU, IEN, MH.
Each play has a separate title-page with the imprint, "by T. N. 1662."; except *The muses looking-glasse*, which has the imprint, "Printed Anno Dom. 1662."

957 - - [Anr.edn.] Oxford: F. Bowman, sold by J. Crosley, Bookseller in Oxford, 1668. 8°. CSmH, CtY, DFo, *DLC, ICN, MH, NIC.
This edition has no punctuation after "Poems" on the general title-page; *The muses looking-glasse* has a one-line imprint; *Amyntas, Aristippus*, and *The jealous lovers* have the title enclosed by single rules; and the first page of *The pedler*, p. 323, has a single row of ornaments at top.

958 - - [Anr.edn.] Oxford: F. Bowman, sold by J. Crosley, Bookseller in Oxford, 1668. 8°. CSmH, CtY, DFo, MH.
This edition has a colon after "Poems" on the general title-page; *The muses looking-glasse* has a two-line imprint; *The pedler*, p. 323, has a double row of ornaments at top; and the title-pages of the other three plays are not enclosed in rules.

- Amyntas; or, The impossible dowry. 1640. In his *Poems,* 1643.

- Aristippus; or, The jovial philosopher. 1652. In his *Poems,* 1652.

RANDOLPH, THOMAS (continued)
The jealous lovers. 1640. In his *Poems,* 1643.

- The muses looking-glasse. 1643. In his *Poems,* 1643.

- The pedler. 1652. See *Aristippus* in his *Poems,* 1652.

959 - Ploutophthalmia ploutogamia: A pleasant comedie, entituled
hey for honesty, down with knavery. Translated by T.
Randolph, augmented and published by F. J[aques]. Printed
in the year 1651. 4°. CSmH, CtY, DFo, DLC, ICU, MH.

960 THE RAPE OF EUROPA BY JUPITER. M. Bennet, 1694.
4°. CSmH.

961 RAVENSCROFT, EDWARD
The anatomist; or, The sham doctor. R. Baldwin, 1697. 4°.
CSmH, CtY, DFo, DLC, ICN, ICU, MH, MWiW-C, MiU,
TxU.

962 - The Canterbury guests; or, A bargain broken. D. Brown and
J. Walthoe, 1695. 4°. CLUC, CSmH, CtY, DFo, DLC,
ICN, ICU, MH, MiU, NjP.

963 - The careless lovers. W. Cademan, 1673. 4°. CLUC, CSmH,
CtY, DLC, MH, MWiW-C, MiU, PU, TxU.

964 - The citizen turn'd gentleman. T. Dring, 1672. 4°. CLUC,
CSmH, CtY, DFo, ICU, MH, MWiW-C, NjP.

965 - - [Anr.edn. with changed title.] Mamamouchi; or, The citizen
turn'd gentleman. T. Dring, 1675. 4°. CSmH.
Dedication "To Lord Arundel."

966 - - [Anr.issue.] CLUC, CSmH, CtY, DFo, *DLC, ICN, ICU,
MH, MiU, TxU.
Dedication "To Prince Rupert."

967 - Dame Dobson; or, The cunning woman. J. Hindmarsh, 1684.
4°. (P 830) CSmH, CtY, DFo, DLC, ICN, MH,
MWiW-C, MiU, NjP, TxU.

968   The English lawyer. J. M. for J. Vade, 1678. 4°. CLUC, CSmH, CtY, DFo, DLC, ICN, ICU, MH, MWiW-C, MiU, NjP, TxU.

969 - The Italian husband. I. Cleave, 1698. 4°. CLUC, CSmH, CtY, DFo, DLC, ICN, ICU, MH, MWiW-C, MiU, NjP, PU, TxU.

970 - King Edgar and Alfreda. M. Turner, 1677. 4°. CSmH, CtY, DFo, DLC, ICN, ICU, MH, MWiW-C, MiU, NjP.

971 - The London cuckolds. J. Hindmarsh, 1682. 4°. CLUC, CSmH, CtY, DFo, DLC, ICN, ICU, MH, MiU, NN, NjP, PU, TxU.

972 - - [Anr.edn.] J. Hindmarsh, 1683. 4°. DFo, ICN, TxU.

973 - - [Anr.edn.] J. Hindmarsh, 1688. 4°. CtY, DFo, DLC, ICN, NjP, TxU.

974 - - [Anr.edn.] H. H., sold by J. Knapton, 1697. 4° . CSmH, CtY, DFo, MH, TxU.

- Mamamouchi. See no. 965.

975 - Scaramouch a philosopher, Harlequin a school-boy, bravo, merchant, and magician. R. Sollers, 1677. 4°. CSmH, CtY, DFo, DLC, ICN, MH, MiU.

976 - Titus Andronicus; or, The rape of Lavinia. J. B. for J. Hindmarsh, 1687. 4°. CSmH, CtY, DFo, DLC, ICN, ICU, MH, MWiW-C, MiU, NjP, PU.

977 - The wrangling lovers; or, The invisible mistress. W. Crook, 1677. 4°. CLUC, CSmH, CtY, DFo, DLC, ICN, MiU. Author's name omitted from title-page.

978 - - [Anr.issue.] CLUC, CSmH, ICU, MH, MWiW-C, TxU. Author's name on title-page.

979 RAWLINS, THOMAS
      Tom Essence; or, The modish wife. T. M. for W. Cademan,
      1677. 4°. (P 832) CLUC, CSmH, CtY, DFo, DLC, ICN,
      MH, MiU, NN, TxU,

980 - Tunbridge-Wells; or, A days courtship. H. Rogers, 1678. 4°.
      (P 833) CSmH, DFo, MH, MiU, TxU.

981 THE REBELLION OF NAPLES; or, The tragedy of Mas-
      senello commonly so called: But rightly Tomaso Aniello di
      Malfa generall of the Neopolitans ... 1647. J. G. and G. B.,
      1649. 8°. CSmH, DFo, DLC, ICU, MH.
      "MDCIL" in imprint.

982 - - [Anr.issue or edn.] 1649. 8°. CtY.
      "MDCLI" in imprint.

983 THE REFORMATION. W. Cademan, 1673. 4°. CLUC,
      CSmH, CtY, DFo, *DLC, *PU, TxU.
      Winged head on title-page.

984 - - [Anr.issue.] CSmH, DFo, ICN, ICU, MH, MiU, TxU.
      Floral ornament on title-page.

985 THE RELIGIOUS-REBELL; or, The pilgrim-prince. Printed,
      Anno Dom. 1671. 4°. CSmH, DFo, DLC, ICN, ICU.

    THE REVENGE. See Betterton, T.

986 REVET, EDWARD
      The town-shifts; or, The suburb-justice. T. Dring and W.
      Cademan, 1671. 4°. CSmH, CtY, DFo, DLC, ICN, ICU,
      MH, MWiW-C, MiU, NjP, TxU.

987 RHODES, RICHARD
      Flora's vagaries. W. Cademan, 1670. 4°. CSmH, CtY, DFo,
      DLC, ICN, ICU, MH, MiU, TxU.

988 - - [Anr.edn.] W. Cademan, 1677. 4°. DFo, MH, TxU.

RIDER, WILLIAM
   The Christmas ordinary. See under title.

989 - The twins. R. Pollard and J. Sweeting, 1655. 4°. CLUC,
   CSmH, CtY, DFo, DLC, ICN, ICU, MH, PU.

A RIGHT PITHY, PLEASANT, AND MERRY COMEDY,
   ENTITULED, GAMMER GURTONS NEEDLE. See
   S., Mr., Mr. of Art.

990 RIVERS, ANTONY
   The traytor. R. Parker and S. Briscoe, 1692. 4°. CSmH,
   DFo, DLC, ICN, ICU, MH, MiU, NN, TxU.

991 ROBIN HOOD AND HIS CREW OF SOULDIERS. J. Davis, 1661. 4°. CSmH.

THE ROMAN VIRGIN. See Webster, J. *Appius and Virginia.*

992 ROMULUS AND HERSILIA; or, The Sabine war. D. Brown
   and T. Benskin, 1683. 4°. (P 836) CSmH, DFo, DLC,
   ICN, ICU, MH, MiU.

993 ROWLEY, WILLIAM
   The birth of Merlin; or, The childe hath found his father.
   T. Johnson for F. Kirkman and H. Marsh, 1662. 4°. CSmH,
   DFo, DLC, MH, MWiW-C, NN, PU.

- The changeling. See Middleton, T. and W. Rowley.

- The Christmas ordinary. See *The Christmas ordinary.*

- A cure for a cuckold. See Webster, J and W. Rowley.

- The excellent comedie, called The old law. See Massinger, P.,
   T. Middleton and W. Rowley.

- The Thracian wonder. See Webster, J. and W. Rowley.

994 ROWLEY, WILLIAM, THOMAS DEKKER and JOHN FORD
   The witch of Edmonton. J. Cottrel for E. Blackmore, 1658.
   4°. (P 841) CSmH, CtY, MH.

995 RUGGLE, GEORGE
   Ignoramus. Ex officina R. D., 1658. 12°. CtY, DFo, MH,
   MiU.

996 - - [Anr.edn.] Ex officina J. R., 1659. 12°. CSmH, DFo.

   - - [Anr.edn. in English.] 1662. See Codrington, R.

997 - - [Anr.edn.] Ex officina J. R., 1668. 12°. CtY, DFo, NIC,
   NjP.

998 - - [Anr.edn.] Impensis G. S., n. d. 12°. DFo.

   - The English lawyer. See Ravenscroft, E.

999 RUTTER, JOSEPH
   The cid. W. Wilson for H. Moseley, 1650. 12°. CSmH,
   CtY, DFo, DLC, ICN, MH, MiU.
   Translated from P. Corneille.

1000 RYMER, THOMAS
   Edgar; or, The English monarch. R. Tonson, 1678. 4°.
   (P 843) CSmH, CtY, DFo, DLC, ICN, ICU, IEN, MH,
   MiU, NjP, TxU.

1001 - - [Anr.issue with changed title.] The English monarch. J.
   Knapton, 1691. 4°. DFo, ICU, MH.
   A re-issue of the 1678 sheets with a cancel title. P 843,
   note.

1002 - - [Anr.issue with original title.] J. Knapton, 1693. 4°.
   "The second edition." P 843, note.

1003 S., MR., MR. of ART
> A right pithy, pleasant, and merry comedy, entituled, Gammer Gurtons needle. T. Johnson, sold by N. Brook, F. Kirkman, T. Johnson, and H. Marsh, 1661. 4°. (G 67b) CSmH, DFo, MWiW-C.

S., J.
> Andromana. See under title.

1004 S., J.
> An excellent comedy, called, the prince of priggs revels; or, The practises of that grand thief captain James Hind. G. Norton, 1651. 4°. CSmH, DFo, DLC.

SACKVILLE, CHARLES, 6th Earl of Dorset
> Pompey the great. See Waller, E.

1005 SADLER, ANTHONY
> The subjects joy for the kings restoration. J. Davis, 1660. 4°. CSmH, CtY, DLC, MH.

1006 ST. SERFE, THOMAS
> Tarugo's wiles; or, The coffee-house. H. Herringman, 1668. 4°. (P 848) CSmH, CtY, DFo, DLC, ICN, ICU, MH, MiU, NjP, TxU.

1007 SAUNDERS, CHARLES
> Tamerlane the great. R. Bentley and M. Magnes, 1681. 4°. (P 854) CLUC, CSmH, CtY, DFo, DLC, ICN, ICU, MH, MWiW-C, MiU, NjP, TxU.

1008 SCOTT, THOMAS
> The mock-marriage. H. Rhodes, J. Harris, and S. Briscoe, 1696. 4°. CLUC, CSmH, DFo, DLC, ICN, ICU, MH, MWiW-C, MiU, NN, NjP, TxU.

1009 - The unhappy kindness; or, A fruitless revenge. H. Rhodes, S. Briscoe, and R. Parker, 1697. 4°. CLUC, CSmH, CtY, DFo, DLC, ICN, ICU, MH, MWiW-C, MiU, NjP, TxU.

1010 SEDLEY, SIR CHARLES
    Antony and Cleopatra. R. Tonson, 1677. 4°. CSmH, CtY, DFo, DLC, ICN, ICU, MH, MWiW-C, NIC, NN, NjP, PU, TxU.

1011 - - [Anr.edn.] R. Bentley, J. Tonson, J. Knapton and S. Manship, 1696. 4°. CLUC, CtY, DFo, DLC, ICN, MH, MiU, PU, TxU.

1012 - Bellamira; or, The mistress. D. Mallet for L. C. and T. Goodwin, 1687. 4°. CLUC, CSmH, CtY, DFo, DLC, ICN, ICU, MH, MWiW-C, MiU, NjP, PU, TxU.

1013 - The Mulberry-garden. H. Herringman, 1668. 4°. (P 856) CLUC, CSmH, CtY, DFo, DLC, ICN, ICU, MH, MWiW-C, MiU, NIC, TxU.

1014 - - [Anr.edn.] H. Herringman, 1675. 4°. CSmH, CtY, DFo, ICN, ICU, MH, MiU, NjP, TxU.

1015 - - [Anr.edn.] 1688. 4°. (CBEL II, 275)

    - Pompey the great. See Waller, E.

    - Tunbridge-Wells. See Rawlins, T.

1016 SENECA, LUCIUS ANNAEUS
    Hippolitus. G.D. for G.Boddington, 1651. 8°. CLUC, CSmH, ICN, ICU, MH.
    Translated by Edmund Prestwich.

1017 - Medea. H. Moseley, 1648. 8°. CLUC, CSmH, CtY, DFo, DLC, ICN, ICU, MH, MWiW-C, NjP, TxU.
    Translated by Edward Sherburne.

1018 - Thyestes. T. R. and N. T. for A. Banks, 1674. 8°. CSmH, DFo, ICU, MH.
    Translated by John Wright.

1019 Troades Englished. W. G. for H. Marsh and P. Dring, 1660.
8°. In Pordage's *Poems*, 1660. CSmH, CtY, ICN, ICU,
PU.
Translated by Samuel Pordage.

1020 - Troades. A. Godbid and J. Playford, for S. Carr, 1679. 8°.
CSmH, DLC, ICN, ICU, MH, MWiW-C, MiU, TxU.
Translated by Edward Sherburne.

1021 - Troas. J. Tonson, 1686. 4°. CSmH, CtY, DFo, DLC, ICU,
MWiW C, MiU, NjP, TxU.
Translated by James Talbot.

1022 SETTLE, ELKANAH
The ambitious slave; or, A generous revenge. A. Roper and
E. Wilkinson, 1694. 4°. CSmH, CtY, DLC, ICN, MH
(imperfect), MiU, NjP, TxU.

1023 - Cambyses King of Persia. W. Cademan, 1671. 4°. CLUC,
CSmH, CtY, DFo, ICN, ICU, MH, MiU, NjP, TxU.

1024 - - [Anr.edn.] W. Cademan, 1672. 4°. CtY, DFo, DLC,
ICU, MH, TxU.

1025 - - [Anr.edn.] W. Cademan, 1675. 4°. CSmH, CtY, DFo,
ICN, ICU, MH, MiU, NIC, TxU.

1026 - - [Anr.edn.] R. Bentley, 1692. 4°. CtY, DFo, DLC, ICN,
IEN, MH, TxU.

1027 - The conquest of China, by the Tartars. T. M. for W. Cademan, 1676. 4°. CLUC, CSmH, CtY, DFo, DLC, ICN,
ICU, MH, NjP.

1028 - Distress'd innocence; or, The princess of Persia. E. J. for A.
Roper, 1691. 4°. CSmH, CtY, DFo, DLC, ICN, MH,
MiU, NN, NjP, TxU.

1029   The empress of Morocco. W. Cademan, 1673. 4°. (M 179ai)
CSmH, DFo, *DLC, ICN, MH, MWiW-C, NjP, *PU,
TxU.
First prologue "by the Lord Lumnley."

1030 - - [Anr.issue.] (M 179aii) CLUC, CSmH, CtY, DFo, MH.
First prologue "by the Earl of Mulgrave."

1031   Entry cancelled.

1032 - - [Anr.edn.] E. Cademan and are to be sold by the Booksellers of London and Westminster, 1687. 4°. (M 179b)
DFo, MH, MiU.

1033 - - [Anr.edn.] B. Lintott, 1698. 4°. (M 179c) CtY, DFo,
IEN, MH, NN, TxU.

1034 - The fairy-queen. J. Tonson, 1692. 4°. *CLUC, DFo, DLC,
ICN, MH, MiU (imperfect), *PU, TxU.
Signed A1, [two disjunct unsigned leaves], [A2], B-G⁴,
H². One unsigned leaf has Preface on recto and verso,
the other, the Prologue on recto.

1035 - - [Anr.issue.] CSmH, CtY, DFo, ICU, MH.
Signed A1, [unsigned leaf], [A2,]B-G⁴,H². The type re-
imposed, so that Prologue is on A2r and Names of persons
on A2v.

1036 - - [Anr.issue.] J. Tonson, 1693. 4°. DFo, MH.

1037 - Fatal love; or, The forc'd inconstancy. W. Cademan, 1680.
4°. CSmH, DFo, DLC, ICN, ICU, MH, MiU, NjP.

1038 - The female prelate; being the history of the life and death of
Pope Joan. W. Cademan, 1680. 4°. CLUC, CSmH, CtY,
DLC, ICN, ICU, MH, MiU, NjP, PU, TxU.

1039 - - [Anr.edn.] J. Watts and J. Knapton, 1689. 4°. CSmH,
DFo, DLC, MH.

114

1040 - - [Anr.issue.] W. C., 1689. 4°. CtY.

1041 - - [Anr.issue.] J. Watts, 1689. 4°. NN.

1042 - Glory's resurrection; being the triumphs of London revived. R. Barnham, 1698. fol. CSmH.

1043 - The heir of Morocco, with the death of Gayland. W. Cademan, 1682. 4°. CSmH, CtY, DFo, DLC, ICN, MiU.

1044 [Anr.edn.] T. Chapman, 1694. 4°. CSmH, CtY, DFo, DLC, ICN, ICU, MH, MiU, NjP, TxU.

1045 - Ibrahim the illustrious bassa. T. M. for W. Cademan, 1677. 4°. (P 870) CLUC, CSmH, CtY DFo, DLC, ICN, ICU, MH, MiU, NjP, PU, TxU.

1046 - - [Anr.edn.] T. Chapman, 1694. 4°. CtY, DFo, ICN, MH, NIC, TxU.

1047 - Love and revenge. W. Cademan, 1675. 4°. MH.
　　　　Lacks post-script on last leaf.

1048 - - [Anr.issue.] CSmH, CtY, DFo, DLC, ICN, ICU, MWiW-C, MiU, *NIC, NjP, TxU.
　　　　Post-script on verso of last leaf.

1049 - The new Athenian comedy. C. Restio, 1693. 4°. CSmII, DLC, ICN, ICU, MH.

1050 - Pastor Fido; or, The faithful shepherd. W. Cademan, 1677. 4°. CLUC, CSmH, CtY, DFo, DLC, ICN, ICU, MH, MWiW-C, NN, NjP, TxU.

1051 - - [Anr.edn.] W. Cademan, sold by R. Bently, 1689. 4°. CSmH, DFo, MH, MiU, TxU.

1052 - - [Anr.edn.] T. Chapman, 1694. 4°. CtY, DFo, ICN, MH, MiU, NIC.

SETTLE, ELKANAH (continued)

1053 Philaster; or, Love lies a bleeding. R. Bentley, 1695. 4°.
(P 51) CLUC, CSmH, DFo, DLC, ICN, MH, MiU.

1054 - The triumphs of London. A. Milbourn for A. Roper, 1691.
4°. CSmH, MH.

1055 - The triumphs of London. J. Orme, sold by R. Taylor, 1692.
4°. CSmH, CtY, DLC, MH.

1056 - The triumphs of London. J. Orme, sold by B. Johnson, 1693.
4°. CSmH.

1057 - The triumphs of London. R. Baldwin, 1694. 4°. British
Museum (?).

1058 - The triumphs of London. J. Wilkins, sold by R. Baldwin,
1695. 4°. British Museum (?).

1059 - The triumphs of London. A. Baldwin, 1699. fol. British
Museum.

1060 - The triumphs of London. R. Barnham, 1700. fol. London
Guildhall.

1061 - The world in the moon. A. Roper, 1697. 4°. CSmH, CtY,
DLC, ICN, ICU, MiU, NjP, TxU.

1062 - - Second edn. A. Roper, 1697. 4°. ICN, MH.

1063 SHADWELL, THOMAS
The works. J. Knapton, 1693. 4°. CLUC, DLC.
General title-page printed to accompany nonce collection
of 17 plays; in the DLC copy all are earlier than 1693
except Timon, 1696, and Libertine, 1697. See also P 873,
notes.

1064 - The amorous bigotte; with The second part of Teague O
Divelly. J. Knapton, 1690. 4°. CLUC, CSmH, CtY, DFo,
DLC, ICN, ICU, MH, MiU, NjP, TxU.

116

SHADWELL, THOMAS (continued)
- - [Anr.edn.] 1691. See his *The Lancashire witches*. 1691.

1065 - Bury-Fair. J. Knapton, 1689. 4°. CLUC, CSmH, CtY, DFo, DLC, ICN, ICU, MH, MWiW-C, MiU, NN, NjP, **TxU.**

1066 - Epsom-Wells. J. M. for H. Herringman, 1673. 4°. CLUC, CSmH, CtY, DFo, DLC, ICN, ICU, MH, MWiW-C, NjP, **TxU.**

1067 - - [Anr.edn.] J. M. for H. Herringman, 1676. 4°. CSmH, CtY, DFo, ICN, ICU, MH, TxU.

1068 - - [Anr.edn.] H. Herringman, sold by R. Bentley, J. Tonson, F. Saunders, and T. Bennet, 1693. 4°. CtY, DFo, DLC, **ICN, ICU, MH.**

1069 - The history of Timon of Athens, the man-hater. J. M. for H. Herringman, 1678. 4°. (P 917) CLUC, CSmH, CtY, *DFo, ICN, ICU, MH, NN, *PU.
[A4v] blank.

1070 - - [Anr.issue.] CSmH, DLC, MiU.
[A4v] "Persons named."

1070a- - [Anr.edn.] 1680. (Summers)

1071 - - [Anr.edn.] J. M. for H. Herringman, sold by J. Knight and F. Saunders, 1688. 4°. CSmH, CtY, DFo, DLC, ICN, ICU, MH, MiU, PU, TxU.

1072 - - [Anr.issue.] J. M. for H. Herringman, sold by R. Bentley, 1688. 4°. CLUC, DFo.

1073 - - [Anr.edn.] T. Warren for H. Herringman, sold by R. Bentley, J. Tonson, F. Saunders, and T. Bennet, 1696. 4°. CSmH, DFo, MH, MiU, TxU.

1074   The humorists. H. Herringman, 1671. 4°. (P 873) CLUC, CSmH, CtY, DFo, DLC, ICN, ICU, MH, MWiW-C, NjP, **TxU.**

1075 - - [Anr.edn.] H. Herringman, sold by F. Saunders and J. Knapton, 1691. 4°. CtY, DFo, DLC, ICN, MH, MiU, **NN.**

1076 - The Lancashire-witches; and, Tegue o Divelly the Irish-priest. J. Starkey, 1682. 4°. CSmH, CtY, DFo, ICU, MH, **NN.**
    Errata on [A3r]. DFo also has variant copy repeating errata list on L2r and omitting the words "the end" at foot of L2v.

1077 - - [Anr.edn.] 1682. 4°. CLUC, CSmH, CtY, DFo, ICN, MH, MWiW-C, NjP, *TxU.
    Reset and errors corrected. No errata.

1078 - - [Anr.issue.] J. Knapton, 1682. 4°. MH.

1079 - - [Anr.edn. with changed title.] The Lancashire witches. The amorous bigot. R.Clavell, J.Robinson, A. and J.Churchill, and J. Knapton, 1691. 4°. CSmH, CtY, DFo, (pt. 1 only), DLC, ICU, NIC, TxU.

1080 - The libertine. T. N. for H. Herringman, 1676. 4°. CLUC, CSmH, CtY, DFo, DLC, ICN, ICU, MH, MWiW-C, MiU, **NjP, TxU.**

1081 - - [Anr.edn.] H.Herringman, sold by R. Bently, J.Tonson, F. Saunders, and J. Bennet, 1692. 4°. CtY, DFo, DLC, **MiU.**

1082 - - [Anr.edn.] T. Warren for H. Herringman, 1697. 4°. **DLC, TxU.**

1083 - The miser. H. Kemp, 1672. 4°. CLUC, CSmH, CtY, DFo, DLC, ICN, TxU.

1084 - - [Anr.issue with changed title.]   A comedy called The miser.
T. Collins and J. Ford, 1672. 4°. CSmH, DFo, TxU.

1085 - - [Anr.edn.]   H. H. and T. C., sold by F. Saunders and J.
Knapton, 1691. 4°. CLUC, CtY, DFo, DLC, ICN, ICU,
MH, MiU, NN, NjP.

1086 - Psyche. T. N. for H. Herringman, 1675. 4°. (P 874)
CSmH, CtY, DFo, ICN, IEN, MWiW-C, NjP, TxU.
"Lower" in imprint; "Countrey" in heading, p. 1.

1087 - - [Anr.edn.] 1675. 4°. CLUC, CSmH, CtY, DFo, DLC,
ICU, MH, MiU, TxU.
"lower" in imprint; "Country" in heading, p. 1. TxU. reports a copy with publisher's name spelled incorrectly.

1088 - - [Anr.edn.] J. M. for H. Herringman, and sold by R. Bentley, 1690. 4°. CtY, DFo, DLC, ICN, ICU, MH, TxU.

1089 - The royal shepherdess. H. Herringman, 1669. 4°. CLUC,
CSmH, DFo, DLC, ICU, MH, MWiW-C, MiU, TxU.

1090 - - [Anr.edn.]   H. Herringman, sold by F. Saunders and J.
Knapton, 1691. 4°. CSmH, CtY, DFo, DLC, ICN, MH,
NjP.

1091 - The scowrers.   J. Knapton, 1691. 4°. (P 875) CLUC,
CSmH, CtY, DFo, DLC, ICN, ICU, MH, MWiW-C, MiU,
NjP, TxU.

1092 - The squire of Alsatia. J. Knapton, 1688. 4°. CLUC, CSmH,
CtY, DFo, DLC, MWiW-C, TxU.
4 p. 1., 88p.

1093 - - [Anr.edn.] 1688. 4°. CLUC, CSmH, DFo, ICN, ICU,
MH, NjP,
4 p. 1., 64p., misnumbered 72.

1094 - - [Anr.edn.] J. Knapton, 1692. 4°. CtY, DFo, MH.

1095 - - [Anr.issue.] J. Knapton, 1693. 4°. CtY, DFo, DLC, MH, TxU.

1096 - - [Anr.edn.] J. Knapton, 1699. 4°. CtY, DFo, ICU, MH.

1097 - The sullen lovers; or, The impertinents. H. Herringman, 1668. 4°. CLUC, CSmH, CtY, DFo, DLC, ICU, MH, MiU, NjP, TxU.

1098 - - [Anr.edn.] H. Herringman, 1670. 4°. CLUC, CSmH, CtY, DFo, ICN, MH, NjP, TxU.

1099 - - [Anr.edn.] H. Herringman, sold by R. Bently, F. Saunders, J. Knapton, and D. Brown, 1693. 4°. CLUC, CtY, DFo, DLC, ICN, MH, TxU.

- The tempest. See Davenant, W.

1100 - A true widow. B. Tooke, 1679. 4°. (P 876) CLUC, CSmH, CtY, DFo, DLC, ICN, ICU, MH, MWiW-C, MiU, NN, NjP, TxU.
       CSmH also has a variant copy with epilogue in different state.

1101 - - [Anr.issue, with title-page and epilogue leaves cancels.] J.Knapton,1689. 4°. CtY, DFo, DLC, TxU.

1102 - The virtuoso. T. N. for H. Herringman, 1676. 4°. CLUC, CSmH, CtY, DFo, DLC, ICN, ICU, MH, MiU, NN (imperfect), TxU.
       Signed A-O⁴.

1103 - - [Anr.edn.] 1676. 4°. (P 877) CLUC, CSmH, CtY, DFo, ICU, MWiW-C, NjP, TxU.
       Signed A-M⁴.

1104 - - [Anr.edn.] H. Herringman, sold by F. Saunders and J. Knapton, 1691. 4°. CtY, DFo, DLC, ICU, MH, MiU, TxU.

SHADWELL, THOMAS (continued)

1105 The volunteers; or, The stock-jobbers. J. Knapton, 1693. 4°.
(P 878) CLUC, CSmH, CtY, DFo, DLC, ICN, ICU, IEN,
MH, MWiW-C, MiU, NjP, PU, TxU.

1106 - The woman-captain. S. Carr, 1680. 4°. (P 879) CLUC,
CSmH (2 variant copies), CtY, DFo, DLC, ICN, ICU,
MH, MWiW-C, MiU, NN, NjP, TxU.

1107 SHAKESPEARE, WILLIAM
Comedies, histories and tragedies. P. Chetwinde, 1663. fol.
(P 908) CLUC, CSmH, CtY, DFo (copies with and with-
out portrait on title-page), MH, MWiW-C, PU.

1108 - - [Anr.issue, with the addition of seven plays.] P.C., 1664.
fol. (P 909) CSmH, CtY, DFo, DLC, ICN, MH,
MWiW-C, MiU, TxU.

1109 - - [Anr.edn.] H. Herringman, E. Brewster, and R. Bentley,
1685. fol. CSmH, CtY, DFo, MH, NN.
See P 910, notes.

1110 - - [Anr.issue.] H. Herringman, E. Brewster, R. Chiswell,
and R. Bentley, 1685. fol. (P 910) CLUC, CSmH, DFo,
TxU.

1111 - - [Anr.issue.] H. Herringman, sold by J. Knight and F.
Saunders, 1685. fol. (P 911) CLUC, CSmH, CtY, DFo,
ICN, NN.

- Antony and Cleopatra. 1677. See Sedley, Sir C.

- - [Anr.edn.] 1678. See Dryden, J. *All for love.*

- Coriolanus. 1682 . See Tate, N. *The ingratitude of a commonwealth.*

- Cymbeline. 1682. See D'Urfey, T. *The injured princess.*

- The history of Timon of Athens, the man-hater. 1678. See
Shadwell, T.

121

1112 Julius Caesar. H. H. Jun. for H. Heringman and R. Bentley, sold by J. Knight and F. Saunders, 1684. 4°. CLUC, CSmH, DFo, MH, TxU.

1113 - - [Anr.edn.] n.d. 4°. CSmH, CtY, DFo, MH.
    In imprint, "Blew Anchor." Catchwords: C1, "Brut;" D1, "Caes. What."

1114 - - [Anr.edn.] n. d. 4°. CSmH, CtY, DFo, MH, PU.
    In imprint, "Blew-Anchor." Catchwords: C1, "Brutus;" D1, "Culp."

1115 - - [Anr.edn.] n.d. 4°. CSmH, DFo, DLC, MH, NN, TxU.
    In imprint, "Blew-Anchor." Catchwords: C1, "Brutus;" D1, "Cal."

1116 - - [Anr.edn.] H. H. Jun for H. Herringman and R. Bentley, sold by J. Knight and F. Saunders. n.d. 4°. CSmH, DFo, MH, MWiW-C.
    In imprint, "Blue Anchor," Catchwords: C1: "[Aside./ Cass."; D1, "And."

1117 - - [Anr.edn.] H. Herringman and R. Bentley, 1691. 4°. (P 886) CSmH, CtY, DFo, MH, MWiW-C, MiU, PU, TxU.

1118 - - [Anr.edn.] R. W., sold by J. Deeve, 1700. 4°. CtY, TxU.

1119 - King Henry IV. With the humours of Sir John Falstaff. R. W., sold by J. Deeve, 1700. 4°. CSmH, CtY, DFo, DLC, MH, MiU, NN, PU, TxU.

- King Henry VI, part I. 1681. See Crowne, J. *Henry the sixth.*

- King Henry VI, part II. 1680. See Crowne, J. *The misery of civil war.*

- King Richard II. 1681. See Tate, N. *The history of . . .*

SHAKESPEARE, WILLIAM (continued)

King Richard III. n.d. See Cibber, C. *The tragicall history of ...*

1120 - Macbeth. W. Cademan, 1673. 4°. CSmH, DFo, MH, PU.

- - [Anr.edn.] 1674. See Davenant, W.

- Measure for measure. 1673. See Davenant, W. *The law against lovers* in his *Works,* 1673.

- - [Anr.edn.] 1700. See Gildon, C.

- A midsummer night's dream. 1661. See *The merry conceited humours of Bottom the weaver.*

- - [Anr.edn.] 1692. See Settle, E. *The fairy-queen: an opera.*

1121 - The most excellent historie of the merchant of Venice. W. Leake, 1652. 4°. (G 172eII) CSmH, DFo, MH, NN.

- Much ado about nothing. 1673. See Davenant, W. *The law against lovers* in his *Works,* 1673.

- Romeo and Juliet. 1680. See Otway, T. *The history and fall of Caius Marius.*

- The taming of the shrew. 1698. See Lacy, J. *Sauny the Scott.*

- The tempest. 1670. See Davenant, W.

- Titus Andronicus; or, The rape of Lavinia. 1687. See Ravenscroft, E.

- The tragedy of Hamlet prince of Denmark. 1676. See Davenant, W.

1122 - The tragoedy of Othello, the Moore of Venice, W.Leak,1655. 4°. CLUC, CSmH, DFo, MH, NN, PU.

1123 - - [Anr.edn.] W. Weak, sold by R. Bentley and M. Magnes, 1681. 4°. (P 893) CLUC, CSmH, DFo, MH, MiU, PU.

1124 - - [Anr.edn.] R. Bentley and S. Magnes, 1687. 4°. CSmH, DFo, MH, MiU, NN.

1125 - - [Anr.edn.] R. Bentley, 1695. 4°. CSmH, CtY, DFo, MH, MWiW-C, MiU, PU.

- Troilus and Cressida. 1679. See Dryden, J.

1126 - True chronicle history of the life and death of King Lear, and his three daughters. Jane Bell, 1655. 4°. (G 265e) CSmH, DFo, MH NN, PU.

- - [Anr.edn.] 1681. See Tate, N. *The history of King Lear.*

SHAW, SAMUEL
Minerva's triumphs. 1680. See his *Words made visible.*

1127 - Poikilophronesis; or, The different humours of men. T. Parkhurst, 1692. 8°. CSmH, DFo.

1128 - Words made visible; or,Grammar and rhetorick accomodated to the lives and manners of men. B.G.for D.Major, sold by D. Brown and T.Orrel,1679. 8°. CSmH, DFo, DLC.
In two parts, second part dated 1678.

1129 - - [Anr.issue.] B. G. for D. Major, 1679. 8°. CSmH.

1130 - - [Anr.edn. with changed title.] Minerva's triumphs; or, Grammar and rhetoric. D. Brown, 1680. 8°. CSmH.

1131 - - [Anr.edn.] 1683. 8°. British Museum.

1132 SHE VENTURES AND HE WINS. H. Rhodes, J. Harris, and S. Briscoe, 1696. 4°. CLUC, CSmH, CtY, DFo, DLC, ICN, ICU, MH, MiU, NjP, TxU.

SHERBURNE, SIR EDWARD
      Medea.   See Seneca, L. A.

  - Troades.   1679.   See Seneca, L. A.

1133 SHIPMAN, THOMAS
      Henry the third of France stabb'd by a fryer.   With The
      fall of the Guise.   B. G. for S. Heyrick, 1678.   4°.   *CSmH,
      *CtY,   DFo, *DLC, ICN, *ICU, *MH, *MWiW-C, *MiU,
      *TxU.
      Signed A⁴, ✤*✤², a², B-L⁴, with three dedications.

1133a- - [Anr.issue.]   1678.   4°.   DFo.
      Re-imposition of the preliminaries retains the dedication
      to Monmouth, the prologue, dramatis personae, and errata.
      Signed A⁴,a²,***²,B-L⁴, with sig.a² cancelling leaves
      A2-4,***1, and Prologue beginning on a2v.

1134 SHIRLEY, JAMES
      Six new playes, viz., The brothers, The sisters, The doubtful
      heir, The imposture, The cardinall, The court secret.   H.
      Robinson and H. Moseley, 1653.   8°.   CLUC, CSmH, CtY,
      DFo, DLC, ICN, ICU, MH, MWiW-C, MiU, NN, NjP,
      PU.
      The court secret is dated 1653; the other plays, 1652.

1135 - Two playes.   The constant maid a comedy and St. Patrick for
      Ireland.   J.Kirton, 1657.   4°.
      A general title, prefixed to the 1640 editions of the plays.
      The constant maid has the imprint cut off; a blank leaf
      replaces title-page of St. Patrick. Huth Cat. 4.1353.

  - Andromana.   See under title.

  - The brothers.   In his *Six new playes*.

  - The cardinal.   In his *Six new playes*.

  - The constant maid.   1640.   In his *Two playes*.

SHIRLEY, JAMES (continued)

1136 - - [Anr.edn. with changed title.]   Love will finde out the way.
J. Cottrel for S. Speed, 1661.   4°.   (P 929)   CSmH, DFo,
DLC, ICU, MH, MWiW-C, NjP, TxU.
Francis Kirkman claims this title, but no copy has been
traced with his imprint.

1137 - - [Anr.issue with cancel title.]   The constant maid; or, Love
will finde out the way.   J. Cotterel for S. Speed, 1667.   4°.
TxU.

- The contention of Ajax and Ulisses, for the armor of Achilles.
In his *Honoria and Mammon.*

- The court secret.   1653.   In his *Six new playes.*

1138 - Cupid and death.   T. W. for J. Crook & J. Baker, 1653.   4°.
(P 924)   CSmH, CtY, ICN.

1139 - - [Anr.edn.]   J. Crooke and J. Playford, 1659.   4°.   CSmH.

- The doubtfull heir.   In his *Six new playes.*

1140 - The gentleman of Venice.   H. Moseley, 1655.   4°.   *CLUC,
*CSmH, *CtY, DFo, *DLC, ICN, *ICU, *MH, *NN.
*TxU.

1141 - - [Anr.edn.]   1655.   8°.

1142 - The grateful servant.   W. Leake, [post 1660.]   4°.   CLUC,
CSmH, DFo, DLC, ICN, MH, NjP, TxU.

1143 - Honoria and Mammon . . . Whereunto is added The contention
of Ajax and Ulisses, for the armour of Achilles.   J. Crook,
1659.   8°.   CLUC, CSmH, CtY, DFo, MH, NjP, TxU.

1144 - - [Anr.issue.]   T. W. for J. Crook, [1659.]   8°.   CSmH,
ICU, MWiW-C.

1145 - - [Anr.issue.]   Printed for the use of the author, [1659.]   8°.
ICN.

SHIRLEY, JAMES (continued)
The imposture. In his *Six new playes*.

1146 - Love tricks; or, The school of complements. R. T. sold by T. Dring Junior, 1667. 4°. CSmH, CtY, DFo, DLC, ICU, **MH.**

- Love will finde out the way. See no.1136.

1147 - The polititian. H.Moseley, 1655. 4°. DFo, MH.

1148 - - [Anr.edn.] H.Moseley,1655. 8°. CLUC, CSmH, DLC, ICN, ICU, MH, TxU.

- St. Patrick for Ireland. In his *Two playes*.

- The sisters. In his *Six new playes*.

- The traytor. 1692. See Rivers, A.

1149 - The triumph of beautie. H.Moseley,1646. 8°. In his *Poems,* 1646. (P 933) CLUC, CSmH, CtY, DFo, ICN, ICU, **MH, TxU.**

1150 - The wedding. W. Leake, 1660. 4°. CSmH, CtY, DFo, ICU, **MH, TxU.**

SIDNAM, JONATHAN. See Bonarelli della Rovere, G. U.

1151 SIDNEY, PHILIP
Her most excellent majestie walking in Wanstead Garden. 1655. fol. (G 152i) In his *The Countesse of Pembrokes Arcadia.* W. Du-Gard: sold by G. Calvert, and T. Pierrepont, 1655. CSmH, CtY, DFo, DLC, ICU, MH, NIC, NN, **TxU.**

1152 - - [Anr.edn.] 1662. fol. (G 152j) In his *The . . . Arcadia.* H. Lloyd for W. Du-Gard; sold by G. Calvert and T. Pierrepont, 1662. DFo, DLC, ICU, MH, MWiW-C, MiU, PU.

SIDNEY, PHILIP (continued)

1153 - - [Anr.edn.] 1674. fol. (G 152k) In his *The . . . Arcadia.*
G. Calvert, 1674. CSmH, DFo, ICN, ICU, IEN, MH, NN,
NjP.

1154 SIMO. 1652. (Harbage).

1155 SMITH, HENRY
The Princess of Parma. J. Wilde, 1699. 4°. (P 949)
CLUC, CSmH, CtY, DFo, DLC, ICN, ICU, MH, MiU,
NN, NjP, TxU.

1156 SMITH, JOHN
Cytherea; or, The enamouring girdle. L. Curtis, 1677. 4°.
CSmH, DFo, DLC, ICN, ICU.

1157 SMYTH, JOHN
Win her and take her; or, Old fools will be medling. J.
Hindmarsh, R. Bently, A. Roper, and R. Taylor, 1691. 4°.
(P 1077) CLUC, CSmH, CtY, DFo, DLC, ICN, MiU,
TxU.

1158 SOPHOCLES
Electra, tr. C. Wase. The Hague: S. Brown, 1649. 8°.
CSmH, CtY, DFo, ICN, MWiW-C, TxU.

1159 SOUTHERNE, THOMAS
The disappointment; or, The mother in fashion. J. Hindmarsh, 1684. 4°. (M 121; P 954) CLUC, CSmM (2
variants), CtY, DFo (2 variants),DLC, ICN, ICU, MH,
MWiW-C, NjP.

1160 - The fatal marriage; or, The innocent adultery. J. Tonson,
1694. 4°. CLUC, CSmH, CtY, DFo, DLC, ICN, MH,
MWiW-C, MiU, NjP, TxU.
P. 25, line 6, "Death."

1161 - - [Anr.edn.] 1694. 4°. (P 955) CSmH, DFo, ICU, MH,
TxU.
P. 25, line 6, "death."

1162   The fate of Capua. B. Tooke, 1700. 4°. (P 956) CLUC,
       CSmH, CtY, DFo, DLC, ICN, ICU, MH, MWiW-C, MiU,
       NjP, TxU.

1163 - The loyal brother; or, The Persian prince. W. Cademan,
       1682. 4°. (P 957) CLUC, CtY, DFo, DLC, ICN, MH,
       MiU, TxU.

1164 - - [Anr.issue.] J. Tonson, 1682. 4°. CSmH.

1165 - The maids last prayer; or, Any, rather than fail. R. Bentley
       and J. Tonson, 1693. 4°. CSmH, DFo, ICN, MH,
       MWiW-C, NjP, TxU.
           P. 1, line 3, "... up-/"

1166 - - [Anr.edn.] 1693. 4°. (P 958) CLUC, CSmH, CtY,
       DFo, DLC, MiU, TxU.
           P. 1, line 3, "... upon/"

1167 - Oroonoko. H. Playford, B. Tooke, and S. Buckley, 1696. 4°.
       (P 959) CLUC, CSmH, CtY, DFo, DLC, ICN, ICU, MH,
       MWiW-C, MiU, NN, NjP, TxU.

1168 - - [Anr.edn.] H. Playford, B. Tooke, and A. Bettesworth,
       1699. 4°. CtY, DFo, MH, TxU.

1169 - - [Anr.issue.] H. Playford, B. Tooke, and R. Bettesworth,
       1699. 4°. DFo.

1170 - - [Anr.edn.] H. Playford and B. Tooke, 1699. 4°. DFo,
       ICU, MH, MiU, NjP, TxU.

1171   Sir Anthony Love; or, The rambling lady. J. Fox and A.
       Roper, 1691. 4°. (P 960) CLUC, CSmH, CtY, DFo,
       DLC, ICN, ICU, MH, MWiW-C, MiU, NjP, TxU.

1172 - - [Anr.edn.] R. Wellington, 1698. 4°. DFo, DLC, ICN,
       MH, NN, TxU.

SOUTHERNE, THOMAS (continued)

1173　The wives excuse; or, Cuckolds make themselves.　W. Freeman, 1692.　4°.　CLUC, CSmH, CtY, DFo, DLC, ICN, ICU, MH, NjP, TxU.

1174 - - [Anr.issue.]　S. Briscoe, 1692.　4°.　(P 962)　CLUC, DFo, DLC, MH, MWiW-C.

1175 SOUTHLAND, THOMAS
　　　Love a la mode.　J. C. for J. Daniel, 1663.　4°.　CtY, DFo, DLC, ICN, ICU, TxU.

- The ungrateful favourite.　See under title.

1176 THE STAGE-PLAYERS COMPLAINT.　In a pleasant dialogue between Cave of the Fortune, and Reed of the Friars.　T. Bates, 1641.　4°.　CSmH, MH, MiU.

STANLEY, THOMAS.　See Aristophanes.　*Clouds.*

1177 STAPYLTON, SIR ROBERT
　　　The slighted maid.　T. Dring, 1663.　4°.　CSmH, CtY, DFo, DLC, MH, MWiW-C, MiU, TxU.
　　　Errors in pagination.

1178 - - [Anr.edn.]　1663.　4°.　CLUC, CSmH, ICN, ICU, MH, TxU.
　　　No errors in pagination.

1179 - The step-mother.　J. Streater, sold by T. Twyford, 1664.　4°.　CSmH, *CtY, DLC, ICU, MH, MiU.
　　　Imprimatur on title-page; errors in pagination.

1180 - - [Anr.edn.]　1664.　4°.　CSmH, DFo, ICN, MWiW-C, TxU.
　　　Type-ornaments on title-page; pagination corrected.

1181 - The tragedie of Hero and Leander.　T. Dring, 1669.　8°.　CLUC, CSmH, CtY, DFo, DLC, ICN, ICU, MH, PU, TxU.

STILL, JOHN.   See S., Mr., Mr. of Art.

1182 STRODE, WILLIAM
The floating island. T. C. for H. Twiford, N. Brooke, and
J. Place, 1655. 4°. CLUC, CSmH, CtY, DFo, DLC, ICN,
ICU, MH, MWiW-C, PU.

1183 SUCKLING, SIR JOHN
Fragmenta aurea. H. Moseley, 1646. 8°. (P 996) *CLUC,
*CSmH, *CtY, *DLC, *MH, *MWiW-C, *MiU, NN,
*NjP, *TxU.
Aglaura has the imprint, "T. W. for H. Moseley;" *Aglaura*
(Act V), "T. Walkley, sold by H. Moseley;" *Goblins*
and *Brennoralt,* "for H. Moseley."

1184 - - [Anr.issue.] 1646. 8°. (P 995) DFo, NN.
Aglaura has the imprint, "Tho. Walkley for H. Moseley."

1185 - - [Anr.edn.]   H. Moseley, 1648.   8°.   (P 997) CLUC,
CSmH, CtY, DFo, ICN, ICU, MH, MWiW-C, NIC, TxU.

1186 - - [Anr.edn.]   H. Moseley, 1658. 8°. CLUC, CSmH, CtY,
DFo, DLC, ICU, IEN, MH, NIC, NN, PU, TxU.

1187 - - [Anr.edn., with changed title.]   The works. H. Herringman, 1676. 8°. CLUC, DFo, TxU.

1188 - - [Anr.edn.]   H.H. sold by R.Bentley, J.Tonson, T.Ben-
net and F. Saunders, 1696. 8°. CLUC, CSmH, CtY, DFo,
ICN, ICU, MH, NIC, NjP.

- Aglaura.   1646.   In his *Fragmenta aurea.*

- Brennoralt.   1646.   In his *Fragmenta aurea.*

1189 - The discontented colonell.   E.G.for F.Eagles-field,n.d.   4°.
CLUC, CSmH, CtY, DFo, DLC, ICN, MH, TxU.

- - [Anr.edn. with changed title.]   Brennoralt.   1646.   In his
Fragmenta aurea.

SUCKLING, SIR JOHN (continued)
The goblins. 1646. In his *Fragmenta aurea.*

1190 - The sad one. H. Moseley, 1659. 8°. In his *The last remains*,
1659. CLUC, CSmH, CtY, DFo, ICN, ICU, MH, TxU.
For explanation of collation see P 998.

- - [Anr.edn.] 1659. 8°. In his *Works,* 1676.

1191 SWEARING-MASTER. N.T.,1681. fol. DFo.

1192 SWINHOE, GILBERT
The tragedy of the unhappy, fair Irene. J. Streater for J.
Place,1658. 4°. CSmH, CtY, MWiW-C, TxU.

1193 - - [Anr.issue.] J. Streater for W. Place, 1658. 4°. CSmH,
DFo, DLC, ICN, ICU, MH.

SYDSERFF, THOMAS. See St. Serfe, T.

T., I. See *Grim the collier of Croyden,* in *Gratiae theatrales.*

TALBOT, JAMES
Troas. See Seneca, L. A.

TASSO, TORQUATO
Aminta. See Dancer, J., and Oldmixon, J.

1194 TATE, NAHUM
Brutus of Alba; or, The enchanted lovers. E. F. for J. Ton-
son, 1678. 4°. (P 1002) CLUC, CSmH, CtY, DFo, DLC,
ICN, ICU MH, NjP, TxU.
CSmH also has variant copy with dedication in different
number of lines.

1195 - Cuckolds-haven; or, An alderman no conjurer. J. H., sold by
E. Poole, 1685. 4°. CSmH, CtY, DFo, DLC, ICN, MH,
MWiW-C, MiU, NjP, TxU.

TATE, NAHUM (continued)

1196 A duke and no duke. H. Bonwicke, 1685. 4°. CLUC,
CSmH, CtY, DFo, DLC, ICN, MH, NjP, TxU.
   CSmH and ICN have separate prologue to this play,
   printed in 1684.

1197 - - [Anr.edn.] H. Bonwicke, 1693. 4°. CSmH, CtY, DFo,
DLC, MH, MiU, NjP, TxU.

1198 - The history of King Lear. E. Flesher, sold by R. Bentley
and M. Magnes, 1681. 4°. (P 918) CLUC, CSmH, CtY,
DFo, DLC, ICN, MH, MWiW-C, MiU.

1199 - - [Anr.edn.] R. Bentley and M. Magnes, 1689. 4°. CSmH,
DFo, MH, PU, TxU.

1200 - - [Anr.edn.] H. Hills for R. Wellington and E. Rumbold,
sold by B. Lintott, 1699. 4°. DFo, MiU.

1201 - The history of King Richard the second. R. Tonson and J.
Tonson, 1681. 4°. (P 919) CSmH, CtY, DFo, DLC,
ICN, ICU, MH, MWiW-C, MiU, PU, TxU.

1202 - - [Anr.issue with changed title.] The Sicilian usurper. J.
Knapton, 1691. 4°. CSmH, DFo, DLC, MH.
   This is a re-issue of the unsold copies of the 1681 edition
   with a new title.

1203 - The ingratitude of a common-wealth; or, The fall of Caius
Martius Coriolanus. T. M. for J. Hindmarsh, 1682. 4°.
CLUC, CSmH, CtY, DFo, DLC, ICN, ICU, MH,
MWiW-C, MiU, NjP, PU, TxU.

1204 - The island-princess. R. H. for W. Canning, 1687. 4°. CLUC,
CSmH, CtY, DFo, ICN, ICU, MH, MWiW-C, NjP, TxU.

1205 - The loyal general. H. Bonwicke, 1680. 4°. CLUC, CSmH,
CtY, DFo, DLC, ICN, MH, NjP, TxU.

1206 TATHAM, JOHN
>
> Aqua triumphalis. T. Childe and L. Parry, 1662. fol. CSmH,
> **CtY, TxU.**

1207 - The distracted state. W. H. for J. Tey, 1651. 4°. CLUC,
CtY, DFo, DLC, ICN, ICU, MH, MiU, PU, TxU.

1208 - Londinium triumphans. W. G. for H. Brome, 1663. 4°.
CSmH.

1209 - Londons glory represented by time, truth and fame. W. Godbid, 1660. 4°. (P 1003) CSmH, ICN, MH.

1210 - London's triumph. H. Brome, 1662. 4°. CSmH.

1211 - London's triumphs. 1657. 4°. British Museum.

1212 - London's triumphs. W. B. for H. Brome, 1664. 4°.

1213 - Londons tryumph, presented by industry and honour. T.
Mabb, 1658. 4°. CSmH.

1214 - London's tryumph. T. Mabb, 1659. 4°. CSmH.

1215 - London's tryumphs. T. Mabb, 1661. 4°. CSmH, CtY.

1216 - Love crowns the end. W. Burden, 1657. 8°. In his *The
mirrour of fancies,* 1657. CSmH, DFo.

1217 - Royal oake. S. G. for R. B., 1660. 4°. CSmH.

1218 - The rump; or, The mirrour of the late times. W. Godbid for
R. Bloome, 1660. 4°. (P 1004) CSmH, CtY, DFo, DLC,
ICN, ICU, MH, MiU, NjP, TxU.

1219 - - [Anr.edn.] 1661. 4°. CSmH, DFo, MH, NjP, TxU.

1220 - The Scots figgaries; or, A knot of knaves. W. H. for J. Tey,
1652. 4°. (P 1005) CSmH, DFo, DLC, MH, MWiW-C,
TxU.
> "Or" is in roman type.

TATHAM, JOHN (continued)

1221 - - [Anr.edn.] 1652. 4°. British Museum.
"Or" is in italic type. See P 1005, note.

1222 TAUBMAN, MATTHEW
London's anniversary festival. 1688. 4°. Bodley, British Museum.

1223 - London's annual triumph. H. Playford, 1685. 4°. CSmH.

1224 - London's great jubilee. L. Curtiss, 1689. 4°. CSmH, DFo.

1225 - London's triumph; or, The goldsmiths jubilee. J. Leake, 1687. fol. CSmH, CtY.

1226 - London's yearly jubilee. H. Playford, 1686. 4°. CSmH.

1227 TAYLOR, JOHN
Englands comfort, and Londons joy. [F. Coules, 1641] 4°. CSmH.
Edition with 13-line title and 4 lines above cut on p.4.

1228 - - [Anr.edn.] Frcncis [sic] Coules, [1641.] 4°. CSmH, Edition with 14-line title and 9 lines above cut on p. 4.

1229 TERENTIUS AFER, PUBLIUS. See also Echard, L.; Hoole, C.
Terence in English . . . Opera ac industria R. B[ernard] J. Legatt, sold by A. Crooke, 1641. 4°. CLUC, CSmH, CtY, DFo, MH, MiU, PU.

1230 THOMSON, THOMAS
The English rogue. W. Thackeray and W. Whitwood, 1668. 4°. CSmH, DLC.

1231 - The life of Mother Shipton. P. Lillicrap, sold by T. Passenger, [1668-1671?] 4°. CSmH.

1232 - - [Anr.issue.] P. Lillicrap, [1668-1671?] 4°. NjP.

THORNY-ABBEY; or, The London-maid. By T.W. 1662.
12°. In *Gratiae theatrales.*

1233 TIMOLEON; or, The revolution. W. Onley for J. Sturton,
1697. 4°. (P 1009) CSmH, CtY, DLC, ICN, ICU, MH,
MiU, TxU.

TITUS; or, The palm of Christian courage. 1644. (Harbage).

1234 TOM TYLER AND HIS WIFE. Printed in the year, 1661.
4°. DFo.
> The second impression. The DFo copy, formerly the
> Huth, contains a three-leaf list of plays. This list, ab-
> stracted from a copy of Goffe's *Careless shepherdes,* 1656,
> is not an integral part of the play.

1235 - - [Anr.issue, with two-line reference on the title-page to
Kirkman's Catalogue of plays.] 1661. 4°. (P 1010)
CSmH, DFo.
> Kirkman's Catalogue is signed A-B⁴.

1236 TOMKIS, THOMAS
> Albumazar. T. Dring, 1658. 4°. (G 330dII) Boston Pub-
> **lic Library.**

1237 - Lingua; or, The combat of the tongue, and the five senses for
superiority. S. Miller, 1657. 8°. (G 239fI) CSmH, CtY,
DFo, ICU, MH, MiU, NjP.
> "A pleasant Comoedy."

1238 - - [Anr.issue.] 1657. 8°. (G 239fII) CSmH.
> "A Serious Comoedy."

1239 Entry cancelled.

1240 THE TRAGEDY OF THAT FAMOUS ROMAN OR-
ATOUR, MARCUS TULLIUS CICERO. R.Cotes for
J.Sweeting,1651. 4°. CSmH, ICN, ICU.

THE TRAGICAL HISTORY OF GUY OF WARWICK.
See J., B.

1241 THE TRIUMPHS OF VIRTUE. A. Roper and R. Wellington, 1697. 4°. CSmH, CtY, DFo, DLC, ICN, ICU, MH, MiU, NjP.

1242 TROTTER, CATHERINE
Agnes de Castro. H. Rhodes, R. Parker, and S. Briscoe, 1696. 4°. CLUC, CSmH, CtY, DFo, DLC, ICN, ICU, MH, MWiW-C, MiU, NjP.

1243 - Fatal friendship. F. Saunders, 1698. 4°. CLUC, CSmH, CtY, DFo, DLC, ICN, ICU, MH, MWiW-C, MiU, NN, TxU.

1244 TUKE, RICHARD
The souls warfare. S.G. for A.Bancks,1672. 4°. CSmH, DFo.

1245 - - [Anr.issue with cancel title.] The divine comedian; or, The right use of plays. S.G. for A.Bancks,1672. 4°. CSmH, DFo.

1246 TUKE, SIR SAMUEL
The adventures of five hours. II. Herringman, 1663. fol. (P 1012) CLUC, CSmH, CtY, DFo, DLC, ICU, MH, MWiW-C, PU, TxU.

1247 - - [Anr.edn.] H. Herringman, 1664. 4°. CSmH, CtY, DFo, MH, MiU, NjP, TxU.

1248 - - [Anr.edn.] T. N. for H. Herringman, 1671. 4°. CSmH, CtY, DFo, ICN, ICU, MH, TxU.

1249 TUTCHIN, JOHN
The unfortunate shepherd. J. Greenwood, 1685. 8°. In his *Poems on several occasions.* CSmH, DLC, ICN, MH.

THE TWO MERRY MILK-MAIDS. See *A pleasant comedy called the two merry milk-maids.*

UNDERHILL, CAVE
Win her and take her. See Smyth, J.

1250 THE UNFORTUNATE USURPER. Printed in the year
1663. 4°. CSmH, CtY, DFo, DLC, ICU, MH.

1251 THE UNGRATEFUL FAVOURITE. J. Cottrel for S.
Speed, 1664. 4°. (P 1017) CLUC, CSmH, DFo, DLC,
TxU.

1252 THE UNNATURAL MOTHER. J. O. for R. Basset, 1698.
4°. CSmH, CtY, DFo, DLC, MH, MiU.

1253 VANBRUGH, SIR JOHN
Aesop. [Part I.] T. Bennet, 1697. 4°. CLUC, CSmH,
CtY, DFo, DLC, ICN, ICU, MH, NjP, PU, TxU.

1254 - Aesop. Part II. T. Bennet, 1697. 4°. CLUC, CSmH,
CtY, DFo, DLC, ICN, ICU, MH, NjP, PU, TxU.

1255 - - [Anr.edn.] [Parts 1 and 2] 1697. 4°. CSmH, DFo,
DLC, TxU.
Part 2 is a re-issue of the separate edition with the title-
page removed.

1256 - The pilgrim... Likewise a prologue, epilogue, dialogue and
masque, written by . . . Mr. Dryden. B. Tooke, 1700.
(M 94a) CLUC, CSmH, CtY, DFo, MH, TxU.
Signed A-G⁴, H².

1257 - - [Anr.issue.] (M 94b) CLUC, CtY, DFo.
Signed A-F⁴, X¹, B-D², plus a blank leaf. A1-F4 are
sheets of the first issue. X1 is the sub-title of Dryden's
Dialogue and Secular Masque, with imprint: B. Tooke,
1700. 2B1-2C2v contain The secular masque; 2D1-2D2v,
the Song of a scholar.

1258 - The provok'd wife. J. O. for R. Wellington and S. Briscoe,
1697. 4°. (P 1020) CLUC, CSmH, CtY, DFo, DLC,
ICN, ICU, MH, MiU, NjP, TxU.

VANBRUGH, SIR JOHN (continued)

1259 - - [Anr.edn.]   R. Wellington, sold by B. Lintott, 1698.   4°.
CtY, DFo, DLC, MH, TxU.

1260 The relapse; or, Virtue in danger.   S. Briscoe, 1697.   4°.
(P 1021)   CLUC, CSmH, CtY, DFo, DLC, ICN, ICU,
MH, MWiW-C, TxU.

1261 - - [Anr.edn.]   S. B., sold by R. Wellington, 1698. 4°. CSmH,
DFo, ICU, MH, NIC, TxU.

VERBRUGGEN, JOHN
A new opera called Brutus of Alba.   See Powell, G.

1262 VILLIERS, GEORGE, Duke of Buckingham
The chances.   A. B. and S. M., sold by L. Curtis, 1682.   4°.
(P 367)   CSmH, CtY, DFo, DLC, MH, TxU.

1263 - - [Anr.edn.]   R. Bentley, 1692.   4°.   CSmH, CtY, DFo,
MH, MiU, TxU.

1264 - The rehearsal.   T. Dring, 1672.   4°.   (M 165a; P 1024)
CLUC, CSmH, CtY, DFo, DLC, ICN, MH, MWiW-C,
NjP.

1265 - - [Anr.edn.]   T. Dring, 1673.   4°.   (M 165b)   CLUC, CtY,
DFo, DLC.

1266 - - [Anr.edn.]   T. Dring, 1675.   4°.   (M 165c)   CLUC, CSmH,
CtY, DFo, ICU, MH.

1267 - - [Anr.edn.]   R. Bentley and S. Magnes, 1683.   4°.   (M 165d)
CLUC, CSmH, DFo, ICN, ICU, MH, MiU, NjP.

1268 - - [Anr.edn.]   T. Dring, sold by J. Newton, 1687.   4°.
(M 165e) CLUC, CSmH, CtY, DFo, MiU, NjP, NN, TxU.

1269 - - [Anr.edn.]   T. Dring, sold by J. Tonson, 1692. 4°. (M 165f)
CLUC, CtY, DFo, MH, NjP.

VINCENT, THOMAS
Paria. 1648. In Hacket, J. *Loiola*.

W., M.
The marriage-broaker. In *Gratiae theatrales*.

W., T.
Thorny-Abbey. In *Gratiae theatrales*.

1270 WALKER, WILLIAM
Victorious love. R. Smith, 1698. 4°. CLUC, CSmH, CtY,
DFo, DLC, ICN, ICU, MiU, NIC, TxU.

1271 WALLER, EDMUND
The maid's tragedy altered. J. Tonson, 1690. 8°. *CLUC,
*CSmH, *CtY, DFo, *DLC, ICN, *MH, *MiU, *NjP,
*NIC, *TxU.
Page 11, line 2, "aboard my Yacht."

1272 - - [Anr.edn.] 1690. 8°. DFo.
Page 11, line 2, "on Board my Yatch."

1273 - - [Anr.edn.] T. Bennet, 1690. 8°. In his *The second part
of Mr. Waller's poems.* (P 1037) CSmH, DFo, MH, NN.

1274 - Pompey the great. H. Herringman, 1664. 4°. (P 1044)
*CLUC, *CSmH, *CtY, DFo, *MH, *MiU, *NjP, *TxU.

1275 - - [Anr.issue.] DFo, ICN.
With added leaf of "Epilogue to the Dutchess..."

1276 THE WANDERING WHORES COMPLAINT. F. Iones,
1663. 4°. Bodley.

WASE, CHRISTOPHER.
Electra. See Sophocles.

1277 WATERHOUSE, DAVID
Cleophilus. Excusum anno dom. 1700. 4°. MH.

1278 WEBSTER, JOHN
    Appius and Virginia. Printed in the year, 1654. 4°. CSmH,
CtY, MH.

1279 - - [Anr.issue.] R.Mariot, 1654. 4°. DFo.

1280 - - [Anr.issue.] Printed in the year,1655. 4°. DLC.

1281 - - [Anr.issue.] H.Moseley,1659. 4°. CSmH, ICN, MH.
1679. 4°. NN.

1282 - - [Anr.issue with changed title.] The Roman virgin or un-
just judge. Printed and sold by most booksellers, 1679.
4°. NN, NjP.

1283   The Dutchesse of Malfy. R. Crofts, n. d. [1657-1664.] 4°.
MH.

1284 - - [Anr.edn.] D. N. and T. C. sold by S. Neale, 1678. 4°.
CSmH, CtY, DFo, ICN, ICU, MH, NjP, TxU.

1285 - The white devil; or, Vittoria Corombona. G. Miller for J.
Playfere and W. Crooke, 1665. 4°. (G 306c) CSmH,
DFo, MH.

1286 - - [Anr.edn. with changed title.] Vittoria Corombona; or,
The white devil. W. Crooke, 1672. 4°. (G 306d) CSmH,
DFo, MH, NN, NjP, TxU.

1287 WEBSTER, JOHN and WILLIAM ROWLEY
    Two new playes: viz. A cure for a cuckold ... The Thracian
wonder. T. Johnson and sold by F. Kirkman, 1661. 4°.
CSmH, NN.

1288 - A cure for a cuckold. T. Johnson, sold by F. Kirkman, 1661.
4°. CLUC, CSmH, CtY, DFo, ICN, MH, NIC, NN, NjP.
Also issued as part of his *Two new playes.*

1289 - - [Anr.issue.] T. Johnson, to be sold by N. Brook and F.
Kirkman and T. Johnson and H. Marsh, 1661. 4°. (P 1061)

WEBSTER, JOHN and WILLIAM ROWLEY (continued)

1290   The Thracian wonder. T. Johnson, sold by F. Kirkman, 1661.
4°. CLUC, CSmH, DFo, DLC, MH, TxU.
Also issued as part of his *Two new playes.*

1291 WESTON, JOHN
The Amazon queen; or, The amours of Thalestris to Alex-
ander the Great. H. Herringman, 1667. 4°. CSmH, CtY,
DFo, DLC, ICN, ICU, IEN, MWiW-C, MiU.

1292 WHITAKER, WILLIAM
The conspiracy; or, The change of government. W. Cade-
man, 1680. 4° CLUC, CSmH, CtY, DFo, DLC, ICN,
ICU, MH, MiU.

1293 WILD, ROBERT
The benefice. R. Janeway, 1689. 4°. CSmH, CtY, *DLC,
MiU.
"FINIS" on p. 67; p. [68] blank.

1294 - - [Anr.edn.] 1689. 4°. CLUC, CSmH, DFo, ICN, ICU,
MH, MWiW-C, NIC, NjP, TxU.
Catch-word on p. 67; added verses and "FINIS" on p. 68.

1295 WILLAN, LEONARD
Astraea; or, True love's myrrour. R. White for H. Cripps
and L. Lloyd, 1651. 8°. CSmH, CtY, DFo, MH, MWiW-C.

1296 - Orgula; or, The fatall error. T. M. for S. and T. Lewis,
1658. 4°. CLUC, CSmH, DFo, ICN, ICU, MH.

1297 WILMOT, JOHN, Earl of Rochester
Sodom. Antwerp[London?], 1684. 8°. (Summers)

1298 - - [Anr.edn.]   B. Crayle and J. Streater, [1689?]   (P 1069,
notes)

1299 - Valentinian. T. Goodwin, 1685. 4°. (M 233; P 1071)
CLUC, CSmH, CtY, DFo, DLC, ICN, ICU, MWiW-C,
MiU, NN, NjP, TxU.

WILMOT, JOHN, Earl of Rochester (continued)

1300 - - [Anr.issue.] H. Herringman, sold by J. Knight & F. Saunders, 1685. 4°. TxU.

1301 - - [Anr.edn.] J. Tonson, 1691. 8°. In his *Poems,* 1691. CLUC, DFo, ICU, MH, MWiW-C.

1302 - - [Anr.edn.] J. Tonson, 1696. 8°. In his *Poems,* 1696. DFo, ICN, ICU, MH, NIC.

1303 WILSON, JOHN
Andronicus Comnenius. J. Starkey, 1664. 4°. CLUC, CSmH, CtY, DFo, DLC, MH, NIC, TxU.

1304 - Belphegor; or, The marriage of the devil. J.L. for L. Meredith, 1691. 4°. CSmH, DFo, DLC, ICN, MiU, NjP, TxU.

1305 - - [Anr.issue.] J. Leake, sold by R. Taylor, 1691. 4°. CSmH, CtY, DFo, DLC, MH, MWiW-C.

1306 - The cheats. G. Bedell, T. Collins, and C. Adams, 1664. 4°. (P 1072) CSmH, CtY, DFo, DLC, MH, MiU, TxU.

1307 - - [Anr.edn.] T. Collins and J. Ford, 1671. 4°. CtY, DFo, MH, PU, TxU.

1308 - - [Anr.edn.] J. Rawlins for J. Wright, M. Pitt, T. Sawbridge, and G. Collins, 1684. 4°. CtY, DFo, ICU, MH, NIC.

1309 - - [Anr.edn.] J. Walthoe, 1693. 4°. CSmH, CtY, DFo, DLC, ICN, MH.

1310 - - [Anr.issue.] For the author, sold by R. Taylor, 1693. 4°. DFo, NIC.

1311 - The projectors. J. Playfere and W. Crook, 1665. 4°. CLUC, CSmH, CtY, DFo.

WILY BEGUILED. See *A pleasant comedie, called Wily beguilde.*

WIN HER AND TAKE HER. See Smyth, J.

1312 WINE, BEERE, ALE, AND TOBACCO. J. B. for J. Grove,
     1658. 4°. CSmH, MH, MWiW-C.

1313 THE WITS; or, Sport upon sport. Part I. H. Marsh, 1662.
     8°. CSmH, DFo, NN.
     27 drolls.

1314 - - [Anr.edn.] E. C. for F. Kirkman, 1672. 8°. CSmH, DFo,
     DLC, ICN MH.

1315 Entry cancelled.

1316 THE WITS; or, Sport upon sport. [Part II.] F. Kirkman,
     1673. 8°. CSmH, DFo, DLC, ICN, ICU, MH, NN, NjP.
     10 drolls.

1317 - - [Anr.edn.] 1673. 4°. CSmH, DFo.

1318 WITS LED BY THE NOSE; or, A poet's revenge. W. Crook,
     1678. 4°. CSmH, CtY, ICN, MH, MiU.

1319 - - [Anr.edn.] L. Curtis, 1678. 4°. CSmH, CtY, DFo,
     MWiW-C.

1320 THE WOMAN TURN'D BULLY. J. C. for T. Dring, 1675.
     4°. CLUC, CSmH, CtY, DFo, DLC, ICN, ICU, MH,
     MWiW-C, MiU, NjP, TxU.

     WRIGHT, JOHN
     Mock-Thyestes, in burlesque. In Seneca, L. A. *Thyestes*.

     - Thyestes. See Seneca, L. A.

1321 WRIGHT, THOMAS
     The female vertuoso's. J. Wilde for R. Vincent, 1693. 4°.
     CLUC, CSmH, CtY, DFo, DLC, ICN, ICU, MH,
     MWiW-C, MiU, NjP, TxU.

1322 WYCHERLEY, WILLIAM
>The country-wife. T. Dring, 1675. 4°. (P 1098) CSmH
>(2 variant copies), CtY, DFo, DLC, MH, MWiW-C.

1323 - - [Anr.edn.] T. Dring, sold by R. Bentley and S. Magnes,
>1683. 4°. CtY, DFo, ICN, ICU, MH, MiU.

1324 - - [Anr.edn.] T. Dring, sold by R. Bentley and S. Magnes,
>1688. 4°. CLUC, DFo, ICN, ICU, MH, MiU, NjP.

1325 - - [Anr.edn.] S. Briscoe and D. Dring, 1695. 4°. *CSmH,
>*CtY, DFo, *MH, *MiU, *TxU.
>In running-title, "Country Wife."

1326 - - [Anr.edn.] 1695. 4°. DFo.
>In running-title, "Country-wife."

1327 - The gentleman dancing-master. J. M. for H. Herringman
>and T. Dring, 1673. 4°. (P 1099) CLUC, CSmH, CtY,
>DFo, DLC, MH, MWiW-C, NjP, TxU.
>Pforzheimer describes two states of the final half-sheet.

1328 - - [Anr.edn.] H. Herringman, sold by T. Dring, R. Bentley,
>J. Tonson, F. Saunders, and T. Bennet, 1693. 4°. CSmH,
>DFo, ICN, ICU, MH, MiU, TxU.

1329 - Love in a wood; or, St. James's park. J. M. for H. Herring-
>man, 1672. 4°. (P 1100) CLUC, CSmH, CtY, DFo,
>DLC, ICN, ICU, MH, MWiW-C, NN, TxU.

1330 - - [Anr.edn.] 1693. 4°. (CBEL II, 410)

1331 - - [Anr.edn.] T. Warren for H. Herringman, sold by R.
>Bentley, J. Tonson, F. Saunders, and T. Bennet, 1694. 4°.
>CSmH, CtY, DFo, ICU, MH, TxU.

1332 - - [Anr.issue.] T. Warren for H. Herringman. 1694. 4°. NjP.

WYCHERLEY, WILLIAM (continued)

1333 - The plain-dealer. T. N. for J. Magnes and R. Bentley, 1677.
   4°. (P 1102) CLUC, CSmH, CtY, DFo, DLC, ICN, MH,
   MWiW-C, NN, TxU.

1334 - - [Anr.edn.] J. Magnes and R. Bentley, 1678. 4°. CSmH,
   CtY, DFo, ICU, MH.
      "Second" edition.

1335 - - [Anr.edn.] R. Bently and M. Magnes, 1677 [i.e. 1678?]
   DFo, MH,
      Third edition.

1336 - - [Anr.edn.] R. Bently and M. Magnes, 1681. CSmH, DFo.

1337 - - [Anr.edn.] R. Bentley and S. Magnes, 1686. 4°. CtY,
   DFo, ICU, MH, MiU.

1338 - - [Anr.edn.] R. Bentley, 1691. 4°. CtY, DFo, MH, MiU,
   TxU.

1339 - - [Anr.edn.] R. Bentley, 1694. 4°. DFo, MH, TxU.

1340 - - [Anr.edn.] R.Wellington and E.Rumbal,1700. 4°. CSmH,
   DFo, ICN.

Supplement

Shortly after the body of the check list had been put in type, military authorities in Washington sanctioned the return from wartime storage of the rare books of the Library of Congress and of the Union Catalogue; about the same time the rare books of the Folger Library were also brought back to Washington. Then as the proof-reading of the check list proceeded, the plays in the Folger collection were for the first time catalogued, and many previously undiscriminated editions and issues came to light. Of these only a few could be included in the body of the check list; the others, together with several additional titles, have been recorded in the following pages, which also provide a number of notes on the bibliographical relations of items included in the body of the check list and several corrections in the location of copies of plays. In consequence, users of the check list will occasionally have to turn to two places in the volume for full information, but the arrangement of the supplementary material by item number will, it is hoped, reduce this inconvenience to a minimum.

It is a matter of regret that time was not available to secure from every cooperating library a record of recent accessions, but in any case it would have been an imposition to ask further aid from the scholars and librarians who had already given so generously of their time. Only such additional copies are reported in this supplement, therefore, as have been used in the compilation of the notes.

Many of the details given below would not have been available but for the kindness and continued assistance of Dr. W. W. Greg, Dr. William Van Lennep, Mr. Herman Mead, Dr. Donald Wing, and my colleagues, Drs. E. E. Willoughby and P. S. Dunkin.

James G. McManaway

147

Supplement

8a BALLET ET MUSIQUE POUR LE DIVERTISSEMENT
DU ROY DE LA GRANDE BRETAGNE. Savoy, T.New-
combe,1674. 4°.

16   Insert DFo.

17   Insert DFo.

28   Insert DFo.

53   Cancel this entry.   A copy at Folger with variant imprint is
dated 1706.

71   Cancel this entry.   This edition probably appeared in 1710.

155   Insert DFo.

172a [Anr.issue.]   1700.   4°.   DFo.
Quire A has vertical chain lines.   A1 is signed "a;" catch-
word on A3v, "RPO."   On A4v is a list of the actors oppo-
site the names of the characters.   In the earlier issue, item
172, quire A has horizontal chain lines; A1 is unsigned;
the catchword on A3v is "PRO-;" and A4v lacks the actors'
names.

173   In this issue, C4 is replaced by a cancel of three leaves signed
C3, C4, C5, containing an additional scene.

191a CARYLL, JOHN
The English princess; or, The death of Richard the III.   T.
Dring,1666.   4°.   Cardiff Library (*teste* Alan Keen).

191b [Anr.issue.]   1666.   4°.   (*teste* Alan Keen).
With two lines added on title-page: "Written in the year
1666 and acted at his Highness the Duke of York's Theatre."

148

212a [Anr.issue.]   Printed in the year 1654.   4°.   TxU.

219   Delete DFo.

231a [Anr.issue.]   1694.   4°.   DFo.
G1 is a cancel; line 19 of G1v reads, "wont" instead of "What."

234   Insert DFo.

237   Delete DFo.

238a [Anr.edn.]   1697.   4°.   DFo.
Also called "Second edition." Line 2 of the Dedication reads "Your Birth you," instead of "Your Birth You" as in 238. The copies at CLUC, MH, NjP, and TxU may belong to either edition.

239   Insert DFo.

COX, ROBERT
The humour of John Swabber. 1656. In his *Actaeon and Diana.*

COX, ROBERT
Rurall sports on the birth-day of the nymph Oenone. 1656. In his *Actaeon and Diana.*

305   Insert DFo.

324a [Anr.issue.]   1656.   4°.   DFo, MH.
Signed, as before, A F⁴,[G²] ; leaf G1, printed partly from the same type as in the first issue, supplies the names of two actors for each of the dramatis personae and on the verso adds the names of the performers of instrumental music.

325a [Anr.issue.]   H.Herringman,1663.   4°.   CSmH, DFo, TxU.
Part I is a re-issue of the edition of 1659 with quire A of the edition of 1663 substituted for the 1659 title-page. Original A4 is also cancelled in some copies. Augmented text is sup-

plied by the insertion of a leaf signed D3 and by cancels; B3 is replaced by B3-[4]; E2 by E2-3; F3-4 by two leaves with text ending on F4v, which had originally been blank. Leaf D3 is found only in the Texas copy. Part II is the **genuine text of 1663.**

326 Signed πA^4,A-F^4,b^2,B-I^4. Only the Morgan Library has the two general title-pages πA1 and A1. CSmH, DFo, and DLC have the πA1 title; CSmH, CtY, and MH have the A1 title. πA1 reads, "The first Part...enlarg'd;"A1, "The First Part ...Enlarg'd."

327a Songs and masques in the Tempest. [?1674.] 4°. DFo.
    A single sheet, signed A^4, without title-page or colophon. Apparently intended for sale at the theatre.

350 A copy in the British Museum has a leaf signed A2 after the normal A2, containing on the recto "The Prologue at Court" and on the verso "The Prologue at the Fryers." Possibly **an inserted leaf.**

356a DIALOGUE CONCERNING WOMEN, IN DEFENCE OF THE SEX. 1691. (Harbage)

367 In some copies, Cole's verses begin on A7v and extend to A8r; in others they are confined at A7v, and A8 is blank.

425 Insert DFo.

428a [Anr.issue.] 1691. 4°. (M91aia) ICU.
    Leaf H2 has "FINIS" at foot of recto and the verso blank. Leaf H3 has blank recto and epilogue on verso, followed by **"FINIS".**

503a [Anr.edn.] Part I. 1694. 4°. DFo.
    This second edition of Part I is signed A-G^4,H^1, instead of A-I^4, and the title-page reads: "As it was acted," instead of "As it is acted." Copies of the first edn. are at DFo and DLC; other copies reported under 503 are unidentified.

503b [Anr.issue.] Part II. 1694. DFo, DLC.
This issue, with four horizontal rules on the title-page, has errors in pagination and probably precedes the other, listed as 503, which lacks the rule following the line ending "Dorset Garden" and which has correct pagination. A copy of 503, Part II, second issue, is at DFo; none at DLC; other copies unidentified.

AN EXCELLENT COMEDY, etc. For "CALLD," read "CALLED."

558a [Anr.edn.] 1649. [? rectius 1660.] 4°. CSmH.
Signed A-D⁴,E², not A-F⁴,G², as in first edn.

FILMER, EDWARD
The unfortunate couple. See Motteux, P.A. *The novelty.*

606a [Anr.edn.] 1698. 4°. DFo, DLC.
The first edn. (M35) ends on L2; this reprint, on K4.

615 Insert DFo.

633a HOLLAND, SAMUEL
Venus and Adonis. 1656. 8°. In *Don Zara del Fogo* by Basilius Musophilus. T.Vere,1656.
See Hazlitt, *Collections and Notes,* 221. This issue precedes 634.

634 This is a later issue of 633a.

HURLADO DE MENDOZA. For "HURLADO," read "HURTADO."

680 For "Ecologue," read "Eclogue."

687,688 According to the *Huth Catalogue,* p.784, item 688 is a reprint with additional text and with the added statement on the title-page, "His Majesty Gracing the triumphs," etc.

688a [Anr.edn. or issue.] n.d.

691,692 According to the *Huth Catalogue,* p.784, item 692 is a reprint with additional text, and with the added statement on the title-page, "The King, Queen, and Duke of York," etc.

697a [Anr.issue.] Wealth out-witted; or, Money is an ass. for the use of the Author, n.d. 4°.
See *Review of English Studies* 1.219.

727a [Anr.issue.] 1690. 4°. DFo.
With shorter form of Dedication, omitting Lee's adaptation of Shakespeare's epitaph, "Reader, for Jesus sake forbear." The 1696 edn. reprints the short form of Dedication.

740a [Anr.issue.] Printed in the year 1689. 4°. DFo.

748 For "Sophinisba," read "Sophonisba."

757 Insert DFo.

767a [Anr.issue.] F.Kirkman,1661. 12°.
Singly or in his *Three new playes,* 1661.

768a [Anr.issue.] F.Kirkman,1661. 12°.
Singly or in his *Three new playes,* 1661.

770a [Anr.issue.] F.Kirkman,1661. 12°.
Singly or in his *Three new playes,* 1661.

790 Dr.Greg reports that Bodley has a copy dedicated to Richard Steadwell.

798 Delete DFo.

849a The masque of Cinthia and Endimion. 1697. 4°.
In G.Powell's *Songs in the new play call'd The imposter* [sic]*defeated; or, A trick to cheat the devil.* [*Teste* Peter Murray Hill]

877a Copies vary in the state of the Prologue leaf. Printed as leaf
K4 and still bound after K3 in some copies, this has blank
recto in the first state and actors' names on the verso. In
the second state, a Prologue appears on the recto. The
note on Pforzheimer 776 describes an unlocated copy in
which the Prologue leaf is replaced by a half-sheet cancel
signed A, with address "To the Reader" on A1 and the
prologue and actors' names on A2.

899a [Anr.issue.] 1673. 4°. DFo.
Differs from 899 in having ornament above the imprint.

900a [Anr.issue.] 1673. 4°. DFo.
Differs from 900 in omitting the alternate title and insert-
ing an ornament above imprint.

941a Songs in the new play call'd The imposter[sic]defeated; or,
A trick to cheat the devil. With The masque of Cinthia
and Endimion, in the last act. Printed in the Year 1697.
4°. [Teste Peter Murray Hill]

954,955 Since the title-page with the imprint of Bowman and Roybould
is a cancel, 955 should precede 954.

961a [Anr.issue.] 1697. 4°.
In this issue, gathering "a" is signed a*, and on a*2v, "Hod-
son" is corrected to "Hodgson."

968a [Anr.issue.] 1678. 4°. TxU.
With ornament on title-page. See Ashley Library IV. 93.

998 Cancel this entry. According to Sir John Hawkins, in his edn.
of Ignoramus, 1787, p.lxxix, two title-pages were printed
for this edn., one without date and the other dated 1707.

1033a The fairy-queen. J.Tonson,1692. 4°.
Signed A², B-G⁴,H², with "Names of the persons" on A2r.
On B1, S.D. begins, "Enter Duke."

1033b [Anr.issue.] 1692. 4°.
    Signed A1,[unsigned leaf],[A2],B-G⁴,H². The unsigned leaf has Prologue on its recto.

1035a [Anr.issue.] 1692. 4°. DFo.
    Differs from 1035 in having outer form of sheet G re-set; on G1, line 4, "Flower," instead of "flower," etc.

1035b [Anr.issue.] 1692. 4°. DFo.
    Differs from 1035a in having sheet B re-set, with alterations; on B1, S.D. begins "Enter Quince."

1036 The title-page is a cancel. Folger copies have additional text on an unsigned leaf inserted after E3 and another inserted after G4.

1038 Insert DFo.

1069 Delete DFo.

1070 Insert DFo.

1087 Delete DFo.

1133b [Anr.issue.] 1678. 4°. DFo .
    Signed A⁴,***²,B-L⁴, with dedications to the Marquis of Dorchester and Roger L'Estrange. This issue apparently preceded 1133 and 1133a.

1139a [Anr.issue.] 1659. 4°. CSmH.
    One issue of 1659 has on the title-page, "with scenes & musick, vocall & instrumental;" the other, "with scenes, variety of dancing, and musick, both vocall & instrumental."

1143 The Wise copy in British Museum has special title-page for *Honoria and Mammon* inserted after A4.

1149 Some copies vary in the punctuation and capitalization of the title-page.

1157a SNELLING, THOMAS
Pharamus siue Libido vindex, Hispanica tragoedia. Oxford, impressi ad utilitatcm A.Pcnneycook,1650. 8°.
Re-issue of *Thibaldus,* 1640, with cancel title.

1175a [Anr.issue.] 1663. 4°. DFo.
With a leaf of verses signed "a" after A4.

1213 There are two variants of this pageant, of which Bodley has both and Huntington only the later. In the earlier, A3 has three rows of ornaments and two paragraphs of Epistle; in the later, one row of ornaments has been removed to make space for a sentence that links the two paragraphs.

1233 Insert DFo.

1271 Remainder copies were bound with unsold copies of *Poems,* 1693, and also issued as part of *Poems,* by H.Herringman, and sold by J. Tonson,1694. See *Grolier Club Catalogue* III. 185.

1272 After the remainder copies of item 1271 were exhausted to make up copies of *Poems,* 1694 (cf.above), the play was reset line for line and enough copies were printed to match the unsold copies of the 1693 *Poems.*

1318 Insert DFo.

WOMEN, IN DEFENCE OF THE SEX. 1691. See Supplement, 356a.

WITHDRAWAL